APOCALYPSE SOON

THE BEGINNING OF THE END

written by
Patrick Heron

edited by
Tom Horn

ISBN

0-9788453-0-7

EAN

978-0-9788453-0-8

© 2007 Patrick Heron

Published by ANOMALOS Publishing LLC.,2870 NE Hogan Road, Gresham, Oregon, USA.

Scripture quotations taken from the HOLY BIBLE, NEW INTERNATIONAL VERSION & KING JAMES VERSION. Copyright © 1973, 1978, 1984 by International Bible Society.

www.nephilimapocalypse.com

First published in Ireland by Blackwater Press, Dublin, Ireland 1997.

Revised and updated, 2007.

Other books by Patrick Heron include the bestselling *The Nephilim and the Pyramid of the Apocalypse* Kensington Publishers, NY, 2007 and *The Apocalypse Generation* Patrick Heron Publishing, Dublin, 2006.

Table of Contents

Preface

A message to the reader:

My wonderful wife Catherine and I have been married now for almost thirty years. She has given me three beautiful daughters for whom I would die. I am willing to stake my daughters lives on the fact that the things that I discuss in this book will come to pass. I believe the events discussed will happen soon. I may be wrong in this, but they will happen someday.

When these things do happen, you will know that we were telling you the truth and that Jesus Christ is the key.

Patrick Heron
Dublin, Ireland, 2007

Introduction

If someone were to come up to you and offer you next Saturday night's lottery numbers before the draw, would you be interested?

The information I am going to provide in the following pages is better than winning the lottery. If you love your family, your parents and your friends, then listen to what I am about to say to you. This information may be the difference between life and death to you and your loved ones.

In the following pages I will endeavour to show that there is hope for those who want it. I believe there is a God who loves us and wants us to know the truth so that we can avoid the catastrophe that lies ahead. He has already told us what is going to happen so that we might be ready for what the future holds. This book is not a weighty tome that will delve into great detail but rather an overview of things to come. I wish to inform you, the reader, of what God says is about to happen. These are not the prophecies of Nostradamus or any self-proclaimed mystic. They are the prophecies of Jesus Christ the son of God and other biblical prophets. Rest assured that if conclusions are presented, they are the result of over thirty years of biblical research and study. These are not my own opinions or ideas but rather are the words given by God and written down by men whom He chose. Later chapters will supply more references and detail and will elaborate on more specific prophecies.

Daniel the prophet from circa 500 BC said that in the last days **knowledge would be increased**. The Book of Revelation has been sealed up to almost everyone including most Bible believing Christians for centuries. Now it is revealing itself to many people.

I believe that God is giving people one last chance to believe before the judgements of God, as revealed in the Book of Revelation, begin to fall on the earth.

You have the opportunity to believe that Jesus Christ is the key to salvation. If you believe then you can be saved. If you are thinking right now that this is unbelievable, then I urge you to put this information away somewhere safe as it will be invaluable to you in the near future.

The majority of the prophecies summarised in the following pages are from the Book of Revelation. This Book, plus some other, pertinent biblical chapters, are included as an appendix for your convenience. Daniel 7 describes the political union of nations that would exist during the Revelation period; these are discussed in detail in chapter 18. Matthew 24 provides a summary by Jesus Christ of events that will occur during the Book of Revelation. Ezekiel 37, 38 and 39 refer to the return of the Jewish people to Palestine and of a future attack upon them from a northern power.

The Book of Revelation, the last book of the Bible, is often called the "Revelation of St. John the Divine." However, its God-given title is in the first verse. **The Revelation of Jesus Christ...** (Revelation 1: 1). The Greek word for revelation is *Apokalupsis*, which literally means "unveiling"—as in the taking away of a veil from the face or the unveiling of a statue. It can also mean the unveiling of future events. Both senses are true here, for in the future all people will see the face of Jesus Christ, and by reading this Book the events of the future can be revealed to you now.

Scripture quotations from the Book of Revelation are taken from the Holy Bible, KJV.

– *Patrick Heron*

chapter 1
DOOMSDAY SCENARIO

As we begin the twenty-first century, the evidence around us would suggest that the World is hurtling headlong into disaster. Daily on TV and in newspapers people are alarmed at what they see. In almost every country in the World lawlessness is on the increase. In the United States of America alone, there are over thirty thousand murders per year and the numbers are rising. There are one thousand five hundred abortions and a thousand teenage pregnancies every day in the US. Rape, violent crime and drug abuse is rising daily and tearing apart the very fabric of society in countries Worldwide. From wars to famines, from nuclear threats to global warming, the evidence of imminent danger surrounds us.

Scientists tell us that the World cannot support the growth in population. The amount of children born in China every three months is equivalent to the whole population of Ireland, about 4 million. By the year 2040, the population of the World will have doubled from what it is today, to almost 12 billion people. At the same time we are beginning to feel the effects of global warming because of the expansion of the hole in the ozone layer. Only ten years ago this hole was the size of Holland; today it is bigger than the whole of Europe. As a result, skin cancer and other related diseases are on the increase in many places and governments are warning people to use sun barrier creams or to stay out of the harmful rays of the sun.

Diseases that we thought we had conquered forever are re-emerging. These include cholera, TB and malaria, which are spreading and killing in great numbers once again. Doctors are alarmed that antibiotics are becoming ineffective because of over-use. The spread of AIDS is rapidly increasing in most countries and is endemic in others. Scientists have predicted that by the year 2020, 60 million people will have full blown AIDS in Africa alone. To date, 25 million have died of AIDS in Africa alone. The threat of a bird flu pandemic has the World medical community on high alert. Add to this the rise in the number of people dying from cancer and heart failure, and we have a gloomy picture of a sick planet that is getting worse.

War and violence surround us. It seems that almost daily our news bulletins show graphic images of nations waging war on their neighbours and other tribes, slaughtering men, women and children with an evil that is hard to contemplate or understand. At present, there are hundreds of conflicts going on all over the globe and the potential for war is evident in the hatred that is simmering beneath the surface in many other areas.

Famine and death stalk the ravaged landscape in the Third World. While the developed World is so rich that we could land men on the moon, millions live in squalor and die for want of a little food and fresh water. It seems the World is like a great ship; while the rich eat, drink and dance on the upper deck, they seem oblivious to the poor and depraved who wallow in the hold beneath, impoverished in the dark night of the soul.

How long can our small planet endure the endless pursuit of profit at the expense of our natural resources? The rain forests are vital to the air that we breathe, yet every five minutes an area the size of a football pitch is cut down in the name of profit. Many of our rivers are so polluted that nothing can live or survive in them, and in certain countries most of the rivers are little more than sewers used only as dumps for industrial waste. In Norway there are lakes so dead that no trace of living organisms or plants can be found in them. This is because of the pollution caused by the environmental disaster of Chernobyl. Traces of nuclear fallout can still be found in trout caught in the small mountain lakes of the West of Ireland because of the same accident. The late Mr. Jacques Cousteau, World renowned marine biologist, recently said that marine life deteriorated by fifty per cent in his lifetime because of the damage done to the oceans by man.

Add to these all the other ills that we witness in society today: the rise of marriage breakup and suicides, murder, widespread crime, pornography, child abuse, lack of discipline in schools, widespread promiscuity and the lack of morals . . .the list goes on.

Can the World avoid the holocaust that appears to be inevitable, or is there any solution to the destruction that seems to be ahead? Is there any hope for mankind, or are we doomed to failure? Jesus Christ and other biblical prophets have told us exactly what is going to happen in the future. Some of the things they said would happen include:

- a huge increase in wars Worldwide
- global famine and hunger
- increases in earthquakes and environmental catastrophes
- rampant diseases causing widespread death
- no drinking water in one-third of all countries
- one-third of all land scorched so no one can grow crops
- a World leader will arise demanding absolute allegiance
- a great army from the East numbering 200 million will slaughter up to 2 billion people
- the greatest battle in all history will begin in a valley called "Megiddo"
- over 3,000 million people will die by the end of this period

On the following pages I will endeavour to show you that there is hope for those who want it. These are the prophecies of Jesus Christ the Son of God and other prophets such as the apostles Matthew, Luke and John.

To most people the Bible is a closed book. We have been told it contains fables and stories of men that bear little meaning to our day and time. Nothing could be further from the truth. The Bible told us that much of what we see happening today would happen. For instance, it was prophesied by Jesus Christ (and by Daniel almost five hundred years before him) that the Jews would be driven out of Palestine and Jerusalem would be trodden down. The Bible prophesied that the Jews would be scattered over the face of the earth and would be despised, persecuted and hated above all nations. It also said that in the latter days (or End Times), God would bring them back to Israel and establish the Jewish Nation once again in Jerusalem. God said He would do this as a sign to other nations. Looking at history we can see the following facts:

- the Roman Empire sacked Jerusalem in AD 70. All the Jewish people were run of out of Israel and have been spread all over the whole World since then—hence the Wandering Jew
- the Jewish people have been despised, persecuted and hated in almost every country they settled in, culminating in the Holocaust in Germany during the Second World War when millions of them perished
- circa AD1900, a few Jewish settlers returned to Israel More followed in the ensuing years
- in 1948 Israel was recognised as a State for the first time almost 1,900 years after the last Jews left Israel and 2,440 years after the prophet Daniel said they would return

There was a noted biblical scholar who lived and preached in Dublin around 1850. His name was Grattan Guinness, and he was related to the famous Guinness family. He said that the Jews would return to Israel and establish their nation once again. He was scorned and laughed at by critics who told him this was impossible as no Jew had lived in the land for over 1,800 years. Today, there are over 6 million Jews in Israel and more are returning all the time from the countries that God prophesied they would return from (see Isaiah 11:11-12).

Jesus Christ and the Hebrew prophets said that there would be a generation of people, somewhere in time, that would witness the signs of the Last Days. They told us that one of the first signs would be the return of the Jews to Israel. At the same time they told us there would be other signs that we were close to the End Times.

We were told that:

- man would develop weapons so powerful that they could destroy all human life
- we would see the emergence of a powerful empire based on a union of democratic countries
- relative peace will sweep the World in the Last Days, however, this is a deceptive peace that will lead to the greatest war in history
- there would be a system of accounting developed that could keep track of the buying and selling of everyone in the World
- there would be a huge increase and explosion in knowledge in the Last Days

Daniel prophesied over 2,500 years ago that the "last" generation would experience a huge increase in knowledge. If we look at the speed of change in the last eighty years or so, this rings true. We have come from the first flimsy plane made by the Wright brothers to landing on the moon, to space shuttles. We have come from horse-drawn carriages to racing cars and from the Pony Express to cyberspace and the internet. It is difficult for us to imagine a God who knows what is going to happen before it does, but this is our limitation. As a noted Bible teacher once said "old Henry understood the Ford, but the Ford did not understand Henry." God is not bound by space and time. When He looks down on us, He sees the past, present and future all at the same time. That is why He was able to prophecy hundreds (if not thousands) of things throughout the Bible, sometimes hundreds and thousands of years before the event occurred. The Book of Revelation is still future yet it was written by John on the Greek island of Patmos almost two thousand years ago.

The first prophecy concerning the Messiah was in Genesis 3:15. All throughout the Old Testament prophecies concerning the coming Messiah are everywhere. For instance, in the last twenty-four hours of Jesus Christ's life, twenty-five specific Old Testament prophecies came to pass.

It was prophesied that the Messiah would be sold for thirty pieces of silver (Zechariah 11:12), betrayed by a friend (Psalms 41:9), forsaken by his disciples (Zechariah 13:7), accused by false witnesses (Psalms 35:11), be dumb before his accusers (Isaiah 53:7) and scourged (Isaiah 50:6). He would have his garments parted (Psalms 22:18), be mocked by his enemies (Psalms 22:7-8), be given vinegar to drink (Psalms 69:21), have not a bone of his body broken (Psalms 34:20) and die with malefactors (Isaiah 53:12). It was also said that the price of his betrayal would be used to buy a potter's field (Zechariah 11:13) and that he should be buried in a rich man's tomb (Isaiah 53:9).

All these prophecies were made from five hundred to one thousand years before Christ was born, yet they were all fulfilled in a twenty-four hour period. Is this coincidence or Divine revelation? Almost one-third of the Bible is prophetic. These are a few quick examples. There are multitudes of them. When you start to put these prophecies together, that's when you begin to see the jigsaw falling into place.

We are now ready to see a summary of what the Bible tells us will occur in the Last Days and the signs that will illustrate that these days are at hand.

chapter 2

THE FUTURE REVEALED

For most people, the Book of Revelation is extremely difficult to understand. A conundrum wrapped in an enigma and surrounded by a paradox! It is the last book in the Bible and is the one
book that has not yet been fulfilled. In other words, it is future. It
tells us what is going to happen to mankind and to the earth, and
its message is very frightening and terrible. Jesus Christ and other
prophets gave us clues and signs as to when these prophecies would
begin to come to pass, and much of what we see happening today
in World events would suggest that we are very close to the beginning of these dreadful times.

Many people might feel that it is negative or wrong to
speak of these horrendous events that are about to befall mankind and the World. To them I would offer this explanation:
if I were to meet you on the street and to warn you not to go
around the next corner as there was a man there with a gun who
is going to shoot you, would this be a negative thing for me to
do? I wish to give you a choice. You can choose to believe and
take appropriate action or else ignore the warning and suffer
the consequence.

If, on the other hand, you are not sure what you believe, then keep this information safe as you may soon find yourself in the midst of the events prophesied in the Book of Revelation. These pages will be evidence that we were telling you the truth: the Bible has the answers, and Jesus Christ is the key to your salvation and that of your family and friends.

I will now give a brief summary of some of the events prophesied in the Book of Revelation. The eight main events that the Bible says will soon happen are as follows:

1. The Rapture
2. The Great Tribulation
3. The Battle of Armageddon
4. The Second Coming of Christ
5. The Millennial Reign of Christ
6. The Final Rebellion of Satan
7. The Judgement of the Wicked
8. The New Heaven and the New Earth

1. The Rapture

The first major event that I believe is soon to happen is called "The Rapture" by many Christians. Briefly, what is going to happen was prophesied by Jesus Christ:

Do not let your hearts be troubled. Trust in God; trust also in me. In my father's house are many rooms; if it were not so, I would have told you. I am going there to prepare a place for you. And if I go and prepare a place for you, I will come back and take you to be with me that you also may be where I am. (John 14:1-3)

Jesus Christ is returning to take out the true Christians both dead and alive. He is going to appear briefly in the clouds. First, all of the true Christians who have died will be raised up, receive new spiritual bodies and meet Jesus Christ in the sky. Then, those of us who have personally received Jesus Christ into our lives and believe God raised him from the dead are leaving too. Yes, strange as it may seem, all of us who are still alive are going to disappear into the sky and join Jesus Christ and the rest of those who have believed in him down through the ages. All of this is going to happen in a split second. One day the World is going to wake up and several million people will have vanished, literally, from the face of the planet.

If you are a believer in Jesus Christ, then this is good news for you. If you are not, then this is extremely bad news for you. If you are still here after the Bible thumpers and fundamentalists disappear, then you must go through the next phase known as "The Great Tribulation." This is going to be a very bad time lasting seven years or a little longer. But all is not lost for you yet!

Jesus Christ gave us clues as to when the Rapture would occur. These are dealt with in more depth in chapter three.

2. The Great Tribulation

Picture this: you turn on the news to find a most disturbing bulletin—millions of people from every corner of the World have mysteriously vanished. You find it hard to believe, but as news from around the World confirms this mass disappearance, a shiver of foreboding and trepidation runs through your body. You feel vulnerable, unsure and perhaps alone. What is going on? Immediately after the Rapture, the World enters into a period known in the

Bible as "The Great Tribulation." Jesus Christ himself talked about this period of time in Matthew 24 and Luke 21.

This period is going to last seven years or slightly longer. In this seven year period the World is going to experience unprecedented pain, sorrow and disaster. There is going to be a huge increase in wars, famines, earthquakes and disease. An incredible phenomenon will also occur. A man will emerge as the greatest leader the World has ever seen. This man will have charm and charisma. He will be the best communicator the World has ever witnessed. This man will persuade almost the whole World that he is the one leader who can rescue the World and the nations and bring about peace on earth. Almost everyone in the World will believe this man's message. However, some will realise that he is not all he is made out to be.

You will find much information about this person in the Word of God. One of the things he will achieve is to broker a peace agreement between Israel and the rest of the Arab nations. He will perform many seemingly incredible miracles, which will cause many people to believe in him. Many will be deceived, but some will not.

This man will pass laws saying that nobody will be able to do business, to buy or sell unless they receive a mark either on their right hand or on their forehead (some biblical commentators think that this might be a computer chip). The worst decision anybody can make is to receive this mark, for God says that whoever receives this mark is eternally doomed.

During the seven years of tribulation, many people will die. There will be no water to drink on one-third of the earth. In another instance one-third of all grass and all trees will be scorched. Also, one-third of the seas will become so polluted that all living creatures and organisms will no longer live. Also during this period up to half of the population of the World, about 3 billion, will suffer death. Many of the people who turn to God and to Jesus Christ will suffer persecution, but there is hope and light at the end of the tunnel. The Great Tribulation will end with the "Battle of Armageddon."

3. The Battle of Armageddon

In Northern Israel, between the sea of Galilee (lake Tiberias) and the river Jordan on the east and the Mediterranean sea on the west, lies the valley of Megiddo. This valley is about thirty miles long and about fifteen miles wide. Because of the topography of the region, many people wanting to travel east from Europe or Africa would funnel through this valley. Also, because of mountain ranges running north-south, many people traveling west from Asia and China have to pass through this fertile plain. Alexander the Great, Caesar, Napoleon, etc., all journeyed through this valley in the past.

At some point (perhaps midway) through the seven year period of tribulation, a very great and powerful army from the north is going to attack the nation of Israel (Many biblical scholars believe this invasion will be a confederacy of Muslim nations led by Russia). However, in the mountains north of Israel, this army will be destroyed.

Israel and all the nations of the World will realise that God saved Israel. This will infuriate the great World leader, and he will go into the Temple in Jerusalem and proclaim that he is the true God. For the remaining three and half years the World will descend into chaos.

This great World leader, the Antichrist, will gather together all the armies of the World to finally push Israel into the sea and kill all Jews once and for all. However, at the valley of Megiddo, this huge army is going to come into conflict with Jesus Christ himself. The greatest battle the World has ever seen will begin at the valley of Megiddo—the crossroads of the World. This time Jesus Christ is coming as King of Kings and Lord of Lords on a white horse. The armies gathered against Israel will be utterly routed at the great "Battle of Armageddon." This will end the period known as the Great Tribulation and usher in the next administration.

4 & 5. *The Second Coming of Christ & the One Thousand Year Reign of Christ*

Remember the words of the Lord's Prayer: *Our Father, who art in heaven; hallowed be thy name. Thy kingdom come; thy will be done on earth, as it is in heaven.*

Well, you cannot have a kingdom without a king and obviously, His will is not being done on earth, nor has it ever been—at least not yet. This passage clearly refers to the future when, it has been promised, Jesus Christ will return to earth personally. He will then set up his kingdom, which will last one thousand years. Jesus Christ will rule his kingdom from Jerusalem. Satan will be bound up for a thousand years, after which time he will be set free for a short period.

During this thousand year reign there will be World peace. If up to half the population of the World is annihilated during the Great Tribulation, then there will still be around 3 billion people on the earth when Jesus Christ returns. That is why it says He will reign with a **rod of iron** and real justice will prevail.

When He returns to the earth He is returning **with his saints.** Thus, they will be helping to administer his justice during this thousand year reign. There will be no more poverty, inequality, famine or disease. It will be a blessed time, where death will be almost unknown. Even the soil and the animal kingdom will change. The lion will eat straw with the ox. The wolf will lie down with the lamb. People who were blind will see. The dumb will speak. The desert will be fertile.

Numbers and numerology have great significance in God's Word. In Genesis 1 we learn that God created the earth (as we know it) in six days. The seventh day was the Lord's Sabbath. This Sabbath was set aside by God as a holy day. Man was to do no work on that day but was to rest and enjoy what God had done for him on the other six days. God rested on the seventh day. It is almost six thousand years from the time of Adam to now: four thousand from Adam to the time of Christ and almost two thousand from Christ to the present. In the future we know that Christ will reign for one thousand years when peace, prosperity, justice and God's will shall be done on earth.

The number of man is six. For six thousand years man has abused the earth and his fellow man. Divine spiritual perfection is seven. It is God's number. In Peter it says that a thousand years is like a day with the Lord and a day is like a thousand years (2 Peter 3:8).

Could it be that the six thousand years gone, plus the one thousand in the future correspond to the six days of creation plus the one day of rest? If this is so, then we are very close to the end of the six thousand years and very close to the start of the one thousand year reign of Christ. I believe this to be the case.

6. *The Final Rebellion of Satan*

Man has enjoyed veritable Paradise for one thousand years. Jesus Christ has reigned over his kingdom with real justice and judgment. There have been no wars, no famine, no earthquakes and no disease. The weather has been perfect. Man lives and enjoys the fruits of his labour. This is how it was meant to be, but there is more.

Satan has been bound for a thousand years. Now he is released again for a short time. During this short release he manages to gather together another huge army who endeavour to wage war against Jesus Christ and his saints. This shows the utter depravity of man—after living under the rule of Jesus Christ in idyllic conditions for so long, he can still choose evil over good. Once again this army is defeated and utterly routed. Now the devil himself, who has deceived the nations, is thrown into the lake of fire where both the Beast and False Prophet have been thrown (Revelation 20:10).

7. *The Final Judgement*

After this there are resurrections and judgments. Everybody who has lived from Old Testament days will be raised up and judged according to what they have done. Anyone whose name is not written in the Book of Life will be thrown into the lake of fire and suffer what is called the Second Death (Revelation 21:8).

8. *The New Heaven and the New Earth*

This is the eighth main event. The number for a new beginning is eight. After all these other prophecies are fulfilled then begins the New Heaven and the New Earth. This is the final fulfillment of God's master plan, God living with his own family—sons and daughters who choose to love Him by their own free will. Everything that has happened previously is but a preface to this main event. God himself will dwell with mankind. They will be His people and God himself will be with them and be their God. He will wipe every tear from their eyes. There will be no more death or mourning or crying or pain, for the old order of things has passed away (see Revelation 21:1-4)

chapter 3
THE RAPTURE-SIGNS OF HIS COMING

In the Roman Catholic Mass, the priest makes a statement: "Christ has died, Christ is risen, Christ will come again." This is about as much as we were ever told about the "Second Coming." Of course, this rhyme goes in one ear and out the other. Most people have not the slightest idea that Jesus Christ is coming back because nobody ever told them about it. Read carefully what is written:

> *For the Lord himself will come down from heaven, with a loud command, with the voice of the archangel, and with the trumpet call of God, and the dead in Christ will rise first. After that, we who are still alive and are left will be caught up together with them in the clouds to meet the Lord in the air. And so we will be with the Lord for ever. (1 Thessalonians 4:16-17)*

In the original Greek text of the Bible the word for *caught up* is *harpazo*. It is from *raptos*, the Latin derivative of *harpazo* that Christians came up with the word *rapture*. So, when Christians talk of the Rapture, they are referring to the first major event that must occur before the events in the Book of Revelation can begin to unfold.

Jesus Christ is going to return briefly to take all those who have believed in Him. In the verses just quoted it tells us that all Christians that have believed since Pentecost and have died will rise first. They will receive a new spiritual body and will meet him in the clouds. Then those of us who are alive and remain here will also get a new spiritual body and be caught up to meet them also in the clouds. We are told in 1 Corinthians 15 that this will happen in **the twinkling of an eye.**

One day soon millions of people will vanish from the face of the earth. Many Christian scholars and believers feel that this event is very near. Jesus Christ, when asked when it would happen, re- plied that **no man knows the day or the hour.** Yet He did not say that we do not know the month or the year. Again, some biblical scholars are saying the Rapture will occur around September or October. They say this because the "Feast of Firstfruits" and the "Feast of Trumpets," as laid down by Moses in the Old Testament, occur in the months of September and October. Also, Jesus Christ was most probably born in September, and Pentecost occurred when the Jews were celebrating the "Feast of Firstfruits."

Nothing that is done by God is haphazard. There is a time and a reason for everything. I believe that the Rapture is very close.

In Matthew 24:3, the disciples came to Jesus Christ and asked him, **What shall be the signs of thy coming and of the end of this age?** A very interesting question. The first thing Jesus mentions in his reply is **take heed that no man deceives you.** Deception is a key word for the tribulation as the great World leader is going to deceive almost the whole World. The disciples asked him what the signs would be.

Here are some of the signs He lists: in the Last Days, **nation would rise up against nation and kingdom against kingdom.** We would hear of **wars and rumours of wars.** There would be **earthquakes and famines in many places** and also **diseases.** People would **die of heart attacks because of what is happening in the World.** The **nations would be in anguish and perplexity at the roaring and tossing of the sea.** There would be **great signs in the heavens.**

Two chapters, Matthew 24 and Luke 21, are specifically speaking about events that will occur during the tribulation. Jesus also said that when we begin to see these things happening we would know that his coming is very near.

Christian people today are perplexed at World news and events. People are concerned that things cannot continue as they are. Every time we look at our television sets we are confronted by incredibly bad news. Wars and rumours of war are rife. The situation in Israel is hard to resolve and appears to be getting closer to conflict than to peace. The terrorist attacks on New York and Washington have precipitated the war in Afghanistan and the bloody mess that is now Iraq. And fundamental Muslims are promising worse to come for all in the West.

In many other countries all over the globe the potential for conflict and war is obvious. It has been said that up to three hundred wars are at present going on all over the World. With the stockpile of nuclear arsenals, mankind has the potential to wipe out the population of the World seven times over. In fact the situation will be so bad in the latter end of the Great Tribulation period that without divine intervention, **there should no flesh be saved** (Matthew 24:22).

In Luke 21:11, Jesus Christ mentioned that when we would see an increase in earthquakes, this was an indication of his imminent return. Earthquakes and other physical calamities are on the increase. Major earthquakes are a phenomenon that are remembered and recorded in the countries where they have occurred. Below is a table of the major earthquakes that have occurred since 1900.

Number of Years major earthquakes

- 1900-1910 (3)
- 1910-1920 (2)
- 1920-1930 (2)
- 1930-1940 (5)
- 1940-1950 (4)
- 1950-1960 (9)
- 1960-1970 (13)
- 1970-1980 (51)
- 1980-1990 (86)

Since 1990, earthquakes in general have dramatically increased in severity and frequency. According to the National Earthquake Information Center, U.S. Geological Survey, the number of earthquakes since 1990 were:

- 1990-2000 (112,044)
- 2000-2010 (347,768 as of 08-29-2006, with several years to go)

Because of the effect of global warming, the weather is getting more peculiar every year. Places that never saw snow now get three feet in one snowfall. Places that received very little rainfall suddenly experience major floods. Rather than getting the usual cold weather here in Ireland in December 2006, it was so warm buds were sprouting and flowers blooming. It seems everywhere in the World the weather is upside down. From earthquakes to hurricanes to tidal waves/tsunamis to extremes of hot or cold weather, it would appear that something peculiar is happening to our weather systems.

Another phenomenon that is obviously on the increase as prophesied is pestilence (disease). The newest and most alarming is AIDS, which is spreading rapidly. Many other diseases are making a comeback such as TB and cholera. There is much concern in the United States of America now because antibiotics are no longer working because of overreliance on them in the past. This leaves the way open for infectious diseases on a mass scale. Other diseases are appearing weekly. Medical authorities in many countries went on high alert recently because of the threat of bird flu. They know that if this infection takes off, it could dwarf the pandemic of 1915, which killed an estimated 50 million people. Some researchers have warned that microwaves from mobile phones and the communication masts cause cancer. We are infecting our cattle and sheep with the unnatural food stuffs we feed them and most of the fruit and vegetables we eat have been dosed with pesticides and other chemicals.

Heart failures were mentioned by Jesus Christ as a sign of his impending return. This is one of the biggest killers in the World at the moment, and yet, it will increase immeasurably when the Great Tribulation arrives.

Another indication He gave of His coming is famine. Little needs to be said about this horrendous reality. Millions are dying yearly of famine in the Third World, and yet, when the situation comes under control in one country, it breaks out somewhere else.

Famine, and death as a result of famine, will increase significantly in the seven years of tribulation. It is quite obvious that what we see now is a precursor to what is to come.

How vulnerable the Western Hemisphere is to a shortage of food. In the tribulation, one-third of the grass and trees will be scorched. Therefore, all the animals and people who live off this land will suffer accordingly. Imagine how long London or Paris or New York would survive without food—not very long!

One-third of the rivers and fountains are going to be polluted, with people dying as a result of drinking the water. No one can survive without clean water. One-third of all sources of clean drinking water will be polluted in the tribulation. Many rivers today are already polluted beyond recovery because of the industrial waste that has been dumped into them. Again, this is a sign of things to come in the near future.

One-third of the seas of the World will **turn to blood** so that no living thing will survive, and one-third of all ships that inhabit these seas will also be destroyed. The deterioration of marine life, which has occurred over the past fifty years or so, is a clear indication of things to come (see Revelation 8:7-8). Jesus Christ said:

> *When these things begin to take place, stand up and lift up your heads, because your redemption is drawing near. (Luke 21:28)*

He also told a parable of the fig tree:

> *Now learn this lesson from the fig tree: As soon as its twigs get tender and its leaves come out, you know that Summer is near. Even so, when you see all these things, you know that it is near, right at the door. (Matthew 24:32-33)*

This reference to the fig tree is a metaphor for Israel. In other words, when you see Israel back in its homeland, know that the time is near. Other hints have been given in other parts of the Word of God as to the "Last Days." Anytime the Bible refers to the "Last Days" it is talking about a very brief period of time before the consummation of that age or period being described. When the "Last Days" or "latter days" or "last times" are used in reference to Israel, it is always referring to the tribulation period and, more specifically, to the last three and half years of that period.

When the phrase "Last Days" or "last times" or "latter days" is used in reference to present day believers, it is always talking about a short time before the Rapture, the appearance of the Son of God in the clouds to take the Christian believers to be with him. The apostle Paul described society as a whole shortly before the Rapture.

People will be lovers of themselves, lovers of money, boastful, proud, abusive, disobedient to their parents, ungrateful, unholy, without love, unforgiving, slanderous, without self-control, brutal, not lovers of the good, treacherous, rash, conceited, lovers of pleasure rather than lovers of God. (2 Timothy 3:1-5)

Mankind today is essentially selfish—"I want it and I want it now!" The race to be at the top of the ladder and make the most money is what is important today. People love money—everybody wants what they see everyone else has, but they don't necessarily want to put in the hard work to earn it. Winning the lottery is most people's dream. Drug dealers live like millionaires by way of their ill-gotten gains. Money is the new status symbol.

Mankind has many boasters who brag about their own achievements. This egomania is very prevalent in all walks of life today. It is the desire to be put on a pedestal and to promote oneself. People are proud—totally independent and self-sufficient without any need for God to supply their needs. They will be **abusive**—we see this now on television and in the movies, on the streets and on the buses. Men, women and children blaspheme the name of God. They **will be unthankful**—how many people pause to thank God for all the good they have, whether it be a meal or all the other blessings we receive. Many people today don't believe in God anyway, so they view everything they have as their right.

In the Last Days, Paul says people will be **without love**, meaning they will become so hardened and so callous that they don't care about other people. **Because lawlessness will increase, the love of many will grow cold** (Matthew 24:12). Their emotions have become so dulled because of sin that they find it hard to respond to natural affection and to give or receive love.

Those who are slanderous are liars. They lie themselves and they accuse others of lying also. They will be **brutal** or uncontrollable. They will be **treacherous**—they will give their word on something and will do the opposite. This is obvious today in politics where people in high places say they will do one thing and then we discover they are doing the opposite. Deception issues from people in high political office as evidenced from the scandals that continue to emerge from politics Worldwide.

Those that are **not lovers of the good** will hate people who talk about Jesus Christ and the truth of the Word of God. People will be **lovers of pleasure rather than lovers of God**. This is certainly true today as everyone all over the globe today just wants to party. They are only interested in sex, drugs and rock and roll.

In Matthew 24:37, Jesus said that in the Last Days it was going to be like it was in the days of Noah before the Flood. In those days they were **eating, drinking, marrying and giving in marriage, up to the day Noah entered the ark.** In short, they were partying all the time. Eating, drinking and having orgies were the order of those days. Noah warned them what was about to happen and they laughed at him. They thought him a fool and an old idiot who was spending seventy or eighty years building a boat up a hill when they had never even seen rain before, let alone a flood!

Well they weren't laughing when the rains began and continued for forty days and nights. Nor were they laughing when the floods began to rise and there was no escape for them or their families. Every single person was drowned—man, woman and child. Yet we cannot seem to learn a lesson from this prophecy. Many people today laugh at Christians. They laugh at those people who tell them that another catastrophe is near, and they had better get their act together. Just as Noah warned the people of impending doom, Jesus Christ is warning us now of the wrath to come in the very near future.

If you have not yet made a decision to receive Jesus Christ as your personal Lord and Saviour, then maybe now is a good time. It's quite simple. All you have to do is believe that Jesus Christ is your Lord and Saviour and that God raised him from the dead. We are given this advice clearly in the Bible:

> *That if thou shalt confess with thy mouth the Lord Jesus, and*
> *believe in your heart that God has raised him from the dead,*
> *thou shalt be saved. (Romans 10:9)*

Ever notice that guy in the crowd behind the goal post at football matches on TV? He is usually holding a big sign saying John 3:16, which is a crucial passage that says the same thing:

For God so loved the World that he gave His only begotten Son that whosoever believes in him should not perish but have everlasting life. (John 3:16)

If you believe this deep down in your heart of hearts, then you are saved. You are now a child of God with his spirit in you. Now you are saved from the wrath to come and instead will be taken out by Jesus Christ when He comes to gather his saints at the Rapture.

Crime, rape, drugs, prostitution, child abuse, adultery and murder are prevalent in every society. Yet, with all this going on it would seem that having a good time, making plenty of money and acquiring faster cars and bigger houses is what is most important. It was once said that religion is the opium of the people. Now it seems sport is the opium of the people. Sports personalities today are among the most important and revered in our society. The top political and religious leaders are rushing around trying to solve the problems of the World. Their work is in vain for they are merely rearranging the deck chairs on the Titanic.

Surely it is obvious to anybody who has eyes to see that the World is on the brink of destruction. Put these Worldwide happenings into context with the prophecies in God's Word regarding the Last Days and it is obvious that we are close to the Great Tribulation. Only the Rapture of the Church of God is preventing this time of wrath. But evidence would suggest that the hour is almost upon us.

Apostasy

There was an interesting comment made on the radio recently. Angela McNamara is an Irish agony aunt who is retiring after forty years in the business. She was asked if she noticed any change in the people of Ireland over the years. She said that the biggest fundamental change she had observed was the de-Christianising of the Irish people. When she was younger, people had a deep rooted spirituality; now it appears this is all but gone. She reckoned people were now more selfish, secular and materialistic and that any sense of God, or good and evil, is gone.

Mr. Desmond Fennell wrote a book about the changes in Ireland over the past fifty years or so. His findings agree with Angela McNamara's—on TV he asked whether Ireland and the Irish people were ready for the changes that would take place in our society in this post-Christian era. When quizzed by the TV host, he said that whereas historically Irish society and its laws were based on Christian laws and values, these have been changing over the years and Ireland was now basing its laws and society on pagan morals and laws. Of course he was roundly criticised by the liberal left panel on the show who said Ireland was a more caring place today than it was in the cold, bleak days of the 40s and 50s.

Last Days

This is evident throughout the globe today. If we take Ireland as a microcosm for the Western Hemisphere, it is abundantly evident that things are going from bad to worse. People are despairing at the levels of crime, drug abuse, murder, rape, etc. This is almost universally proportional to the rejection of Christian morals and values over the past thirty years or so. Are we surprised at this decline in Western civilisation? No, for this is another indication that we are perilously close to the Rapture and to the start of the Great Tribulation. Neither God, Jesus Christ nor Paul ever said the World was going to get better until finally all hunger, war and evil have been eradicated. Rather they stated the opposite.

They said the World would get increasingly worse until culminating in the seven years of Great Tribulation where people would eventually destroy themselves were it not for divine intervention. Believers in Jesus Christ who know these prophecies do not despair at the demise of the World. Instead, we observe the fulfilling of prophecy in World events and rejoice at the imminence of the Rapture.

chapter 4
UFOS AND ALIENS

After the Rapture, when millions of true Christians vanish from the face of the earth, Satan will have to come up with a credible explanation. He knows his time is short and is already laying the groundwork of his plan. Thousands of people around the World believe they have been abducted by aliens. Hundreds of thousands have reported sightings of UFOs. Many prominent leaders in World history have reported seeing UFOs or believe in their existence. These include Senator Barry Goldwater, Jimmy Carter, Prince Philip, General Douglas MacArthur, John Kennedy and Ronald Regan. Indeed Ronald Regan mentioned UFOs on eighteen different occasions while President of the United States.

Hardly a week goes by without another sighting of a UFO. Many of our TV programs are UFO and alien related. For instance, *Stargate*, *Dark Angel* and *Buffy the Vampire Slayer* are huge favourites. Some of the biggest box office hits of recent times were movies like *ET*, *Close Encounters of the Third Kind* and *War of the Worlds*. More and more scientists are studying psychic and paranormal phenomena and lending credence to their existence. Only a few years ago people who talked of such things as UFOs and aliens would be considered insane. Today their doctrine is accepted as real. The Antichrist may say that aliens or UFOs are responsible for the abduction of millions of people after the Rapture occurs.

I have no doubt that there are such things as UFOs, and I'm sure people have seen them. Again we look to Jesus Christ to find a clue.

And there will be...fearful events and great signs from heaven.
(Luke 21:11)

Technically speaking, heaven is a distant habitation where, we are told, God and Jesus Christ and some other spiritual beings reside (this is discussed in chapter 9). Heaven can also mean the atmosphere around the earth. When Jesus said **you will see signs in the heavens**, I believe UFOs are what he was talking about. I do not believe that these UFOs are driven by aliens from another planet or galaxy.

No, I believe these luminous objects are being sent by Satan, the devil, to fool people. Furthermore, if people are being abducted, it is not aliens who are abducting them but rather demons. Remember, the devil has a lot of power. It is not difficult for him to make what look like spacecrafts appear in the air. Also, He has a host of spirit beings, who rebelled with him, at his disposal (spirit beings are discussed more fully in chapter 11). Satan's original name was Lucifer. Lucifer means bearer of light, or shining one, so he knows the secrets of light and knows how to appear as an **angel of light** (2 Corinthians 11:14).

I spoke to two people who saw a UFO near Phoenix in Arizona. There was a crowd of people looking at this object at the same time.

They said it was like a giant luminous, translucent jellyfish that hovered in the air from which light seemed to emanate. It stayed there for many minutes, and then sped away. It is no problem for the devil to make these "flying objects" appear. Nor for him to make statues move or have the sun (apparently) dance in the sky.

It is interesting to note that these objects are usually described as "bright" or "luminous" given the meaning of Lucifer. He is out to deceive and fool people, and so far millions around the World are being fooled. A man called Whitley Streiber wrote one of the best selling books of the 1980s called *Communion* where he tells of his personal abduction by so-called aliens. This is what he says about his encounter:

Increasingly I felt as if I was entering a struggle for my soul, my essence, or whatever part of me might have reference to the eternal. So far the word demon had never been spoken among the scientists and doctors who were working with me. And why should it have been? We were beyond such things. We were a group of atheists and agnostics, far too sophisticated to be concerned with such archaic ideas as demons and angels…I felt an absolutely indescribable sense of menace. It was hell on earth to be there, and yet I couldn't move, couldn't cry out and couldn't get away. I lay as still as death, suffering inner agonies. Whatever was there seemed so monstrously ugly, so filthy and dark and sinister. Of course they were demons. They had to be, and they were here and I couldn't get away. I couldn't save my poor family. I still remember that thing crouching there, so terribly ugly, its arms and legs like the limbs of a great insect, its eyes glaring at me.

This hardly sounds like a description of benevolent aliens from space, come to help man straighten out the World but rather an evil spiritual force bent on death and destruction, with Satan as their head and a myriad of demons at his command.

According to the Bible, there are only two sets of powers in the World. God, Jesus Christ and their millions of spirit beings known as angels are on one side; Lucifer, the devil and the angels (one-third) he took with him when he fell from grace are on the other. There are no aliens or other beings in outer space trying to make contact with us, just the devil and his evil spirits. Since people don't know the Bible, he is succeeding in tricking millions into believing in UFOs and aliens. Don't say you haven't been warned.

If you are reading this after the disappearance of millions of Bible fundamentalists, remember one fact: the first thing Jesus Christ said to watch for, after the Rapture, is deception. The one thing that those of us who disappear have in common is that we all believed that Jesus Christ is the Son of God, and we made him Lord in our lives. Therefore, if many so-called Christian leaders are still here on earth after the Rapture, then they are not and were not real believers in Christ. So do not be taken in by what they say.

After the Rapture there will be a great World leader who will have very wonderful and plausible explanations for what has happened. He has been in the business of deception for a very long time. Even though this leader has incredible charisma and charm and is the greatest communicator of all time, do not be deceived. This man is going to be so persuasive, he is going to make John F. Kennedy look like a second-rate politician.

At this moment in time there are incredible changes taking place in technology on a daily basis. The only thing that is constant is the rate of change. When I was a boy we watched *Flash Gordon* with amazement. Now, in this age of space shuttles and satellites, fibre optics and the internet, what seemed mere flight of fancy is now a reality. "Beam me up Scotty" may not now seem so far-fetched, and I would not be surprised if "beam me up" is part of the explanation of the Antichrist after the Rapture.

There will be many **signs and wonders** performed by the Antichrist and other people during the tribulation period. These signs and wonders will be done in order to sway your mind and get you to believe the doctrine of the great leader who will emerge in this time. Do not be deceived; deception will be the order of your day if the Rapture has already occurred.

The Epistles of John, of which there are three, are beautifully written. In the first epistle, John tells us that a symptom of the Last Days would be a prevalent **spirit of Antichrist**. This spirit of Antichrist manifests itself in the denigration of the death and resurrection of Christ and truthfulness of the Word.

There are many books in vogue at the moment that do just this. *The Da Vinci Code* is a prime example. Usually they are based on theories that directly contradict the written Word of God. The authors of such books are interviewed by people who lack the detailed knowledge of the Word to adequately debate with them. Although these authors are generally very well educated and well spoken, they quote scripture out of context to suit their own argument. This is exactly what the devil did when he tempted Jesus Christ to jump from a high temple (see Luke 4:9-11). Quoting from Psalms the devil reminded Jesus it was written that **He will command his angels concerning you to guard you carefully**. Jesus replied that it also said, **Do not put the Lord your God to the test**.

Most people have little or no knowledge of the Bible and, thus, are prone to believing what they hear. The persuasive people who attempt to rebut the veracity of the Word are the forerunners of the Antichrist (who will soon be making his appearance). This is another verification of the accuracy of prophecy. These people are liars, and the devil is the father of all lies. They are out to deceive.

The following pages provide a summary of some of the events we are told will come to pass in the Book of Revelation. These prophecies are frightening in their detail and reality. However, to be forewarned is to be forearmed. Once you have the knowledge of what will happen in the future, then you can plan accordingly.

chapter 5
POLITICAL AND MILITARY MANUEVERS

Have you ever noticed how Israel and Palestine are constantly in the news? When an incident occurs that relates to these two communities, it receives wide media coverage. Other important news stories, such as floods and hurricanes—which claim hundreds of lives—are given less attention.

There are over 6 million Jews in Israel today. They are surrounded by about 250 million Arabs. The key to World peace is the Arab/Israel situation. We are told in Revelation that the great leader, also known as the Antichrist, will broker a peace treaty between Israel and the Arab nations. This will mark the beginning of the seven year period known as the Great Tribulation. The Middle East is also the centre of the World geographically, and the valley of Megiddo is the scene for the future battles to determine which powers will rule the World.

The Valley of Megiddo is also called Armageddon. It is in the north of Palestine and stretches from Mount Carmel forty miles across to the sea of Galilee. Napoleon marched across this plain and said it was the greatest natural battlefield in the World. It is to this battlefield God will bring the greatest marching armies the World has ever seen, to see who will rule the World in the future.

During the tribulation, four great power blocks will emerge. As the prophecies concerning these powers unfold, you will see how present day military and political activities are getting ready to play out these final scenes. All these scenarios are dealt with in detail by other learned biblical scholars. Here I will give you but a brief summary of events and situations.

The "king of the south" biblically has always referred to Egypt. The "king of the north" many biblical scholars now agree, is Russia. Never before in biblical history was this great power mentioned. Two thousand years ago Russia was not a great power. But today only the United States of America is more powerful in military terms. The "kings of the east" were never discussed in old biblical times. But in the future the "kings of the east" amass an army 200 million strong. China recently announced that they could assemble an army of this size at short notice. The other power spoken of in the Last Days is the **beast with ten horns**. A future powerful global Empire consisting of a confederacy of ten unions will make up this Beast with ten horns. Europe will be a central player is this future global confederacy. (This idea is discussed in chapter 18). Revelation 17:13 says the beast will emerge as leader of this union. So it is apparent that the great World leader known as the **Antichrist** or **son of perdition** will emerge as the leader of this global Union. It is feasible that any military incursions made by this Union would have the backing of the United States of America, as it is the most powerful country in the World at present.

About halfway through the Great Tribulation, three and a half years after the Rapture of the Christians, the kings of the south, i.e.

a Pan-Arab confederacy led by Egypt, will move on Palestine and Israel, with the backing and approval of Russia. At the same time, the Russians with some of her Arab allies will move on the Jews from the North and Jerusalem will be destroyed. Two-thirds of the Jewish people will be killed. One-third will flee into hiding in the wilderness.

After the Russian and Arab confederacies swarm over Palestine and destroy Jerusalem, they will retreat to the mountains north of Israel. Then these great armies will be destroyed just as Sodom and Gomorrah were destroyed, by fire and brimstone. When the remainder of the Jews see this vast army destroyed, they will recognise that God has avenged them, and they will turn to Him once again. The destruction of the military might of Russia and these other Arab nations will cause a power vacuum in the Middle East. The leader of the global Union will work fast. He will move into Palestine with the power of the Union's military might behind him. He will declare that he is the true God and rightful Emperor of the World.

The "kings of the east" will start to come into the picture about this time with their army of 200 million men. The whole World will be in chaos during these seven years of the Great Tribulation. Whatever will happen in the East we can only surmise, but prophecy tells us that this huge army kills one-third of the population of the World during this time. The area known to us today as Asia, China and the Far East contains more than a third of the earth's population. After destroying this vast amount of people in the Orient, the "kings of the east" will turn their attention towards the West.

A final conflict seems the inevitable conclusion. All the powers of the Western hemisphere will line up to meet with a huge army from the East. The scene of the final battle will be Armageddon. The greatest battle in the history of the World will be about to take place, but before they can engage in conflict, to see for once and for all who will rule the World, something happens:

> *Immediately after the tribulation of those days shall the sun be darkened, and the moon shall not give her light, and the stars shall fall from heaven, and the powers of the heavens shall be shaken. (Matthew 24:29)*

> *And then shall appear the sign of the Son of man in heaven. (v. 30)*

In the Old Testament, God appeared as a pillar of light in the sky for Israel to follow.

> *Then I saw the beast, and the kings of the earth, and their armies gathered together to make war against the rider on the horse and his army. (Revelation 19:19)*

So these huge armies will join together to fight against the Lord Jesus Christ. I believe the battle that then begins will result in a nuclear holocaust that will engulf the whole World. But this time Jesus will not be coming as a servant on a donkey. When He returns to earth next time, He will come on a white horse, and He will rule with a rod of iron. Next time, He will come as King of Kings and Lord of Lords. He will destroy these armies with the sword that goes out of his mouth. We are told that the rout that begins at Armageddon will be so vicious, the blood will reach to the top of the horses bridles to a distance of two hundred miles away (Revelation 14:19, 20). Then Christ will descend again on the Mount of Olives to begin his reign on this earth for one thousand years. Then and only then, will be fulfilled the words uttered almost two thousand years ago: *Thy kingdom come; thy will be done on earth as it is in heaven.*

Many other events will occur during the seven year period of the Wrath of God—the Great Tribulation. We know that wars, famine, earthquakes, storms and diseases will be multiplied a thousandfold during this era. Many people will turn to God and to Jesus Christ and receive salvation in those days. Many of these believers will lose their lives as a consequence of their belief in the Lord Jesus Christ. However, the few years of this time of great sorrow will seem like a mere shadow compared with the glory that shall be ours as we enjoy eternal life with the risen Christ Jesus.

Is it not interesting that in Old Testament times, Russia was not mentioned in Scripture? Neither was Europe nor the Orient. Yet it is only in the last generation that Russia has become a World power. The same could be said of Europe and the Oriental powers. In bygone years they had no relevance or significance to the events surrounding Israel. God knew that in the future these great military powers would come into play. Through the Bible He informs us of the role these power blocks will play in the near future.

Reading newspapers and magazines today it is clear that all these players are aligning themselves for this future conflict. The Arab nations look to Russia for backing. China has broken links with Russia and is a more independent Communist country now. Europe is consolidating its economic sphere and expanding its membership to include East European countries. The stage is being set for the final drama. Israel is constantly at odds with her Arab neighbours, and the World leaders are constantly seeking real and lasting peace there. The stage is set for the final act.

chapter 6
FOUR HORSEMEN OF THE APOCALYPSE

The image of the four horsemen of the Apocalypse has inspired both wonder and dread. Although many of us have seen pictures or illustrations of four different coloured horses ridden by demonic looking characters, few have understood their significance. The interpretation as to what the four horsemen represent is quite simple. When the disciples asked Jesus what the signs would be of the end of this age:

> *Jesus answered: Watch out that no one deceive you. For many will come in my name, claiming, "I am the Christ," and will deceive many. You will hear of wars and rumours of wars, but see to it that you are not alarmed. Nation will rise against nation, and kingdom against kingdom. There will be famines and earthquakes in various places. (Matthew 24:4-7)*

We have the key here, in the above four verses, to the meaning of the four horsemen of the Apocalypse. The Word of God cannot contradict itself. Careful study and examination will always provide the student with the correct solution.

I watched as the Lamb opened the first of the seven seals. Then I heard one of the four living creatures say in a voice like thunder "Come!" I looked, and there before me was a white horse! Its rider held a bow, and he rode out as a conqueror bent on conquest. (Revelation 6:1-2)

Jesus Christ is the Lamb of God. When John the Baptist saw Jesus Christ he said, **Behold the Lamb of God who takes away the sin of the World.** Jesus Christ is the only one worthy to open these seals. Jesus Christ described these very times to his disciples in Matthew 24; therefore, there can be no doubt as to their meaning and reality. The first thing He said was to watch out for false Christs and many who would deceive. We are also to watch out for the one special deceiver who would say, **I am the Messiah**, as he shall deceive many (Matthew 24:5).

The first rider on a white horse, therefore, must be the Antichrist who, it is promised, will rise to World fame and will deceive many into believing that he is the Messiah who will save the World. Later in Revelation it tells us that Jesus Christ will return as King of Kings and Lord of Lords on a white horse. One of the characteristics of Satan is that he always endeavours to counterfeit what the true God does. Thus, the Antichrist who will rise to govern the nations of the World during the seven years of tribulation is depicted as going forth to conquer these nations on a white horse. He will deceive the nations into believing his message, and he will make war with the saints of God and overcome them.

When the Lamb opened the second seal, I heard the second living creature say "Come!" Then another horse came out, a fiery red one. Its rider was given power to take peace from the earth and

to make men slay each other. To him was given a large sword.
(Revelation 6:3-4)

This relates directly to the Lord's words in Matthew 24:6-7 when He said, **And ye shall hear of wars and rumours of wars... nation shall rise against nation, and kingdom against kingdom.** This points to a general breakup of the nations of the World. In the tribulation period, conflicts throughout the World will multiply. Many places today are very close to conflict. In Lebanon we had the Hezbollah wage a proxy war on Israel with the backing of Iran and Syria. Iran says Israel should be wiped off the map. The invasion to liberate Iraq and establish democracy has turned into a bloody civil war with hundreds being killed weekly and no end in sight. In Britain there is potential for conflict with the different ethnic groups. In the United States of America there are areas in many of the cities that are virtually lawless and where the police do not go. In almost every country today there is the potential for bloodshed on some scale. All these conflicts will be realised in the near future when the rider on the red horse goes forth to make war.

> *When the Lamb opened the third seal, I heard the living crea-*
> *ture say, "Come!" I looked, and there before me was a black*
> *horse! Its rider was holding a pair of scales in his hand. Then*
> *I heard what sounded like a voice among the four living crea-*
> *tures, saying "A quart of wheat for a day's wages, and three*
> *quarts of barley for a day's wages, and do not damage the oil*
> *and the wine!" (Revelation 6:5-6)*

This relates to Matthew 24: 7 where the Lord Jesus Christ said, **And there shall be famines.** Black always denotes famine. Bread by weight always denotes scarcity. What we have here is a great scarcity of food throughout the World. In the original context of this prophecy, the price of wheat (bread) and barley are vastly inflated. Famines have often been foretold (from Genesis onwards, 2 Kings 6:25, 7: 1, Acts 11:28) and have happened. This famine in Revelation will also take place. We have witnessed famine on a daily scale on our TV screens over the years. Yet when the rider on the black horse is released, famine will be experienced on a far wider scale.

We in the Western hemisphere think that famine could never affect us today because farming methods are so efficient. Yet all that is required to trigger such a situation would be a collapse of the financial markets. Many economists today predict just such a collapse in our economic systems. If we do not learn from history, we are bound to repeat it. Financial crashes happened in Germany in the 1920s, the US in the 1930s and Argentina in the 1960s. All these were stable economies with strong industrial bases. Yet overnight money was not worth the paper it was printed on. By whatever cause, famine is going to be Worldwide, and many millions will starve as a result.

> *When the Lamb opened the fourth seal, I heard the voice of the fourth living creature say, "Come!" I looked, and there before me was a pale horse! Its rider was named Death, and Hades was following close behind him. They were given power over a fourth of the earth to kill by sword, famine and plague, and by the wild beasts of the earth. (Revelation 6:7,8)*

This opening of the fourth seal is the fourth judgement mentioned by Jesus Christ in Matthew 24:7, pestilences (diseases). The word in the original Greek text is *thanatos* meaning *death*. It is used as a metonymy. For instance, we called the plague that raged in Europe in the fourteenth century the "black death" as the appearance of a black sores on the armpits indicated the arrival of the disease and then certain death. Pestilences, wars and famines are the agencies used by death, and these are always followed by a common result—the grave.

Pestilence is already rampant throughout the World today. AIDS is one disease we hear much about, but cancer, heroin addiction, BSE, cholera, TB, etc., are all on the increase. Hardly a day goes by without news of the disastrous effects of these diseases. The threatening bird flu pandemic would make AIDS look like small-fry. Yet what the World is experiencing today will be magnified and increased a hundredfold in the seven years of tribulation.

To sum up, the meaning of the four riders of the Apocalypse is quite clear. They are an expansion of Jesus Christ's statement, in Matthew 27:4-7, where He warned first of the great deceiver who would rise to rule the World. This is the rider who goes out to conquer the World on a white horse, counterfeiting the Lord Jesus Christ who will return on a white horse as King of Kings at the end of the seven year period. The red horse and his rider is war. Wars will increase to a huge extent as nation will rise against nation, and kingdom shall rise against kingdom. When the red horse and its rider go forth in the near future, potential trouble spots will erupt into wars such as have never been experienced before. The black horse and its rider are famine, which often follow the ravages and devastation of war. The pale horse represents the diseases that are the consequence of wars and famines. Death and the grave are in constant train.

The Book of Revelation describes many other catastrophes, for example, Revelation 8:7-11 tells us of the poisoning of all drinking water in one-third of the World. It also describes the pollution of one-third of the seas of the earth and the scorching of one-third of all trees and grass. Revelation 6:12 says the whole solar system will unravel, and all the earth will suffer a huge convulsion (earthquake) that will move every mountain and island out of its place.

These prophecies were spoken of in many other places in the Old and New Testament. This particular one, concerning the heavens and the earth, are spoken of in Isaiah 34:1-5 and Isaiah 8: 6-13 and mentioned by Jesus Christ himself in Matthew 24:35.

When the figures mentioned throughout the Book of Revelation are added up, there is a terrible conclusion. Almost half of all people will die in the Great Tribulation. I read recently that the population of the World is almost 6 billion. This means that up to 3,000 million people will perish in these seven years. This seven year period is also known as **the day of judgement of God** and **the great day of His wrath**. This is when God's judgement and wrath are poured out on the earth because of man's rejection of God and of His Messiah.

Please do not take my word for it. When God and Jesus Christ say something will happen, you can be assured it will.

I tell you the truth, until heaven and earth disappear, not the smallest letter, not the least stroke of a pen, will by any means disappear from the Law until everything is accomplished. (Matthew 5:18)

chapter 7
THE BEAST AND THE FALSE PROPHET

The Book of Revelation tells us there will be three powerful influences at work in the tribulation. These are the Dragon, the Beast and the False Prophet. The Dragon is Satan—the devil. It is he who gives power to the Beast—the Antichrist who will rise to a position of power and great authority in the World. Then there is the False Prophet. He is a man who will also receive great power and authority, but his sphere of influence will be religious. Whereas the Beast will manifest himself as the great political ruler, full of charm, wit and seeming wisdom, the False Prophet will give his backing to the Antichrist and urge people to trust in him and in his solutions. The False Prophet will speak with guile and subtlety and as crafty and deceitful as a dragon.

Both the Antichrist and the False Prophet will work for and be in the direct control of the devil. The False Prophet, as a powerful religious leader, will perform wonders and miracles. As a result, many will believe in him and do homage and worship him. The False Prophet will work alongside the Antichrist in order to deceive the whole World. In fact, in Matthew 24:24, it says that these two are so persuasive that, if it were possible, they would deceive the very elect of God.

I expect that the political leader, called in scripture the Antichrist, will arrive on the World scene very soon after the Rapture of the Church. This man will be the greatest, most charming, most lovable man ever to appear on your TV screens. He will con almost the whole World into his way of thinking. I believe that television will be used by him to sway the hearts and minds of people all around the globe.

An amazing thing is going to happen in order to bring the Antichrist to prominence. We are told in Revelation 13:3-4 that the Antichrist will receive a head wound and die. However, a great miracle occurs when this man, in view of the whole World, will be healed of this deadly wound. As a result the whole World will worship this man and worship the one who gave power to him. We do not know the specific details of this seemingly great miracle. But we do know that this man will be killed in view of the whole World. He will then be resurrected from death by the deceiving power of Satan himself. This is a counterfeit resurrection.

His partner, the False Prophet, will be convincing the religious element in society. He will encourage everyone to worship the Antichrist and to pledge themselves to his new way of thinking. Between the Antichrist and the False Prophet, they will present a new religion that has nothing to do with Jesus Christ and the true God. In fact the Antichrist and the False Prophet will be very outspoken against Jesus Christ and his God. They will urge people to believe in themselves, to believe that they have great powers within themselves and, indeed, to believe that they are themselves Gods. As a result, people will delight in this great man (the Antichrist). He will be seen as a benefactor of the whole World. The False Prophet will urge people to do homage to the Antichrist.

I believe we are already seeing the roots of this new all inclusive religion. The New Age movement has been growing in influence and acceptance throughout the World. Its main tenet is that mankind has the power of good and evil within itself and that we do not need a God or Jesus Christ to show us the way. Much of what is preached and practised over the airwaves today has its basis in New Age doctrine, which has resulted in the World at large turning away from Christian principles and values.

In the new religion, God is forgotten and mankind is exalted. It is a combination of wisdom, science, progress and philanthropy, combined with all that panders to the lowest instincts of mankind. We can see this every day in the media. Things that were once taboo are now everyday occurrences on TV and radio. An example of this New Age doctrine is, for instance, the promotion of promiscuity and sex outside marriage, adultery, divorce, homosexuality and lesbianism, one parent families and reliance on the state as provider. Blood sports such as hunting and fishing are condemned, but abortion is condoned. Those who advocate this New Age doctrine roundly attack Christians and anyone who speaks on God's behalf. They label them Bible thumpers, fundamentalists and fanatics, and they embrace anyone or anything that is opposed to God and that represents paganism and hedonism. They support rights for prisoners and the rights of minority groups but do not accept Christians. They promote the individual, but they do not want parents to discipline their children by smacking. Another manifestation of this paganism is the way in which many people use rings and pins to mutilate their bodies by piercing.

I believe this new religion is replacing our laws and society, which have been based for centuries on Mosaic laws and Christian principles. In a very short amount of time almost the whole World has changed before our very eyes. It seems that we are becoming a global Sodom and Gomorrah. This is evidenced by the fact that only a short time ago a law was passed in Holland that allows children of twelve years old to have sex with older people of any age, as long as they (the child) consent.

This mode of thinking has been called "liberal left." Proponents seem to think that as we are in the twenty-first century, we should be intelligent and educated enough to forget old-fashioned systems and embrace the new age of enlightenment. Pornographic videos and magazines are permitted because adults are mature enough to decide themselves what they should or should not watch. The New Age doctrine encourages the relaxing of censorship laws. The fact is that none of this thinking is new.

Sodom and Gomorrah, the Greek Empire and the Roman Empire all reached this age of "enlightenment." They all became so rich and powerful that they allowed liberal laws and sexual freedom to flourish. As a result, the people became so decadent that the whole system collapsed and the empires ended in ruin. The liberal left intelligentsia think they know better than everybody else. Woe betide anyone who challenges or speaks against them or dares to question their reasoning. Thus, they are not so liberal, as "liberal" means to be open-minded. In actuality, they are very narrow-minded when someone takes an opposite point of view. However, in the seven years of tribulation, a new godless, universal religion will be propounded by the Antichrist and the False Prophet. What we are seeing today may be the forerunner of this New Age religion that will flourish in the tribulation.

chapter 8
666 - THE MARK OF THE BEAST

One element of the Book of Revelation that most people are aware of is **the mark of the Beast**. It has been the basis of many horror movies, books and album covers. The number 666 is used to instill fear and wonder. Revelation 13 says that in the future there will be a system of accounting whereby the buying and selling of everyone in the World will be traceable. This would have been impossible up to a few years ago. But the technology exists today whereby computers can track the financial transactions of individuals all around the globe. Is it not amazing that this prophecy was written almost two thousand years ago; yet, in our generation it has become feasible?

Everyone will be given a choice to make. Either you take this mark and side with the Antichrist or, if you do not take the mark, then you suffer the consequences.

He also forced everyone, small and great, rich and poor, free and slave, to receive a mark on his right hand or on his fore-head, so that no-one could buy or sell unless he had the mark, which is the name of the beast or the number of his name. This

calls for wisdom. If anyone has insight, let him calculate the
number of the beast, for it is man's number. His number is
666. (Revelation 13:16-18)

This choice will be the choice between life and death, for we are told that whoever takes this mark and worships the Antichrist will suffer eternal damnation. We do not know exactly what this mark will be. But we were told over two thousand years ago that this would take place during the tribulation. Up to just a few years ago, the idea of putting a mark on everyone in the whole World seemed far-fetched. But we have seen huge advances in technology in recent years. Now, by the use of computers, it is very feasible to keep track of what people buy and sell all over the globe. Therefore, in our day and age, it is not difficult to imagine an identification system that could track the buying and selling of every individual on the planet.

Even as I write, plastic cards are replacing the use of cash. Plastic cards operate from tiny microchips. This microchip contains all the information regarding the owner's account. Some scholars believe that the mark of the Beast could be a microchip inserted just under the skin of the right hand or on the forehead. Already, many dogs and cats and pet birds have an identification chip implanted in them. And by the year 2009, all pets in the US must, by law, have this chip inserted. It seems society is already being primed to accept a chip in humans as the next step. Of course we do not know for sure if this will be the case. But we do know that anyone who does not accept this mark will have great difficulty doing business in those days.

Nobody can buy or sell unless they receive this mark. So people will have a choice to make. Either they go along with this great leader and pledge themselves to his way of thinking or be alienated. The Antichrist will hunt down those people who reject him and turn to God and His Christ. Many of the saints will die in this era because of their allegiance to God and Jesus Christ. But to those who accept the mark of the beast and worship the Antichrist, be warned:

> If anyone worships the beast and his image and receives his mark on the forehead or on the hand, he, too, will drink of the wine of God's fury, which has been poured full strength into the cup of his wrath. He will be tormented with burning sulphur in the presence of the holy angels and of the Lamb. And the smoke of their torment rises for ever and ever. There is no rest day or night for those who worship the beast and his image, or for anyone who receives the mark of his name. (Revelation 14:9-11)

Although it may seem that receiving the mark of the Beast is an innocuous decision, there is obviously more to it than that. It seems that whoever makes this decision is giving total allegiance to the Antichrist. They are saying that they whole-heartedly endorse the Antichrist and the dragon (Satan) that gave him the power. Even though this political leader openly curses God and Jesus Christ, people will worship him and support him. Even though he declares war on the saints and kills them, the whole World not only agrees with him but will openly worship Lucifer as well! This will surely happen as will all the other prophecies that God has revealed to us. "The most important trick the devil ever pulled was to convince the World that he doesn't exist!" That is what one of the characters in the movie The Usual Suspects said during an interrogation. For the most part, people still do not believe in the existence of Satan.

If millions of people have already disappeared off the face of the earth, then you will have the evidence of the truth happening before your eyes. For shortly after the Rapture takes place, this man will arise on the World's stage to begin his deception. Do not be deceived.

chapter 9

THE TWO WITNESSES

Many things that are written in the Book of Revelation seem almost unbelievable. But there again many things throughout the whole Bible seem unbelievable. There are also those who choose not to believe in many of the miracles performed by Jesus Christ while on earth. Some of the better known miracles are: the opening of the Red Sea for the children of Israel to escape and the collapse of the banks of water to drown the pursuing Egyptians, the destruction of the two cities of Sodom and Gomorrah by fire and brimstone, the transformation of Lot's wife into a pillar of salt because she disobeyed the two angels by turning to see what was happening, the changing of water into wine at the wedding feast of Cana, the walking of Jesus on water and calming a storm and the feeding of the five thousand with a few loaves and fishes. Also, in the Book of the Acts of the Apostles, many incredible miracles occurred. In Acts 3 Peter healed a beggar who had been a cripple since birth. Multitudes used to lie on the roadside so that the mere shadow of Peter might fall on them, causing them to be healed. The whole Bible is filled with the miracles of God that appear unbelievable to the ordinary man.

In the same way, the account of the two witnesses in Revelation 11:3-14 is very mysterious. In the latter half of the seven years of tribulation, God will raise up two special men who will prophecy and speak on his behalf. These two men will be endowed with great power from God. If anyone tries to kill them, he or she will be devoured by fire and thus killed. This occurred before in 2 Kings 1:10. Also they will have the power to prevent rain from falling (1 Kings 17:1) and to turn the waters into blood as happened before (Exodus 7:19) and to cause plagues to occur (Exodus 19:15). Nobody will be able to injure them for the three and a half years of their testimony.

When they have finished their work, they will be attacked and killed by the "Beast." Their dead bodies will be left on the streets of Jerusalem for all the World to see for three and a half days. The ungodly people of the earth rejoice and celebrate the death of these two prophets because they were such a thorn in the side of the unbelieving powers. Furthermore, it says all the people and nations rejoice at these deaths. Of course, with modern day satellite communications that have access to the entire globe, this concept is quite believable. As this was written almost two thousand years ago, it shows prophetic foresight.

After their corpses are left in the street for three and a half days, the spirit of life will enter into them again, and they will stand up on their feet. At this spectacle, great fear will fall upon everyone that sees them. The two witnesses are going to be raised up from the dead by the power of God, just as Jesus Christ was raised up (in those days a person had to be dead for three days and three nights in order to be legally pronounced dead).

After they are raised from the dead they will be taken up into heaven in a cloud as their enemies look on (see Acts 1:9). Within an hour of this Ascension, there will be a huge earthquake in which seven thousand men will be killed. Everyone else watching these developments will become terrified. Some day in the (near) future, these two men will appear on the earth and fulfill their mission—in spite of those who disbelieve.

chapter 10
PEACE AT LAST

No peace will prevail until the Prince of Peace returns and establishes His kingdom and rules with a rod of iron. Then and only then will real justice and real peace reign. The Bible does not say the World will improve until Jesus Christ returns. In fact, it says the World will get worse and become more immoral and more Godless and lawless. It is no wonder that on a daily basis we see the World degenerating. There is more pollution in our seas and rivers. The air we breathe is being contaminated. The devastation of the rain forests means that there is less oxygen entering the atmosphere. Disease is killing millions around the World despite our advances in medicine and technology. The same can be said of heart failure, which is one of the biggest killers in the World today.

Yet Jesus Christ told us to expect an increase in all these things. He told us in Matthew 24 and Luke 21 that when we see all these things begin to get worse we should get ready—for our redemption is close. Most people today are frightened and bewildered at the mounting chaos that surround them. Those of us who know Jesus Christ and the Word of God are provided with an assurance and comfort that we will soon see our Saviour face-to-face, for we have been **saved from the wrath to come** (Romans 5:9, 1 Thessalonians 1:10).

If you are reading this before the Rapture and tribulation has started and if you want to learn more, I suggest getting a Bible (the New International Version is recommended). Just go to Matthew 1 and start to read. In Matthew 7: 7 it says **ask and thou shalt receive, seek and you shall find, knock and the door shall be opened unto you**. That is an absolute promise to you from Jesus Christ. So while you are reading, please ask God in your own heart to teach you from His Word. All you have to do is seek, and you shall find. You will be amazed at what has been sitting under our noses all these years, and nobody told us. As you read and begin to put the pieces of the jigsaw together, God will thrill your heart as He opens up the Word of Life to you. God loves you and wants you to know and experience this love. People will hurt you and let you down, but God and Jesus Christ will never hurt you or disappoint you.

Soon after Pentecost, when many people became Christians, they were so convinced of the return of Christ that they used to go up on their flat-roofed houses to wait for him. In Acts 1:10 the two angels said, **this same Jesus will come in like manner as you have seen him go into heaven**. The original disciples thought He was returning any day, and, thus, they went up on their roofs to watch out for him. That was almost two thousand years ago, so we are two thousand years closer to His coming right now. When He returns:

> *The Lord himself shall descend from heaven with a shout, with the voice of the archangel, and with the trump of God; and the dead in Christ shall rise first. Then we which are alive and remain shall be caught up together with them in the clouds, to*

meet the Lord in the air; and so shall we ever be with the Lord.
(I Thessalonians 4:16, 17)

In the Gospel of John 14:2-3, Jesus says **I go to prepare a place for you…and I will come again and take you unto myself.** So when He returns briefly in the clouds and snatches us out, we are going to this place He has been preparing for the past two thousand years. I am looking forward to seeing what He looks like in person. I am also curious as to what our resting place will be like. We are only spending a short time there with Him. After a seven year hiatus, while the World goes through the chaos of the Great Tribulation, we shall return with the Lord Jesus Christ to begin the thousand year reign of Christ upon earth. Thus, there is something great to look forward to.

What exactly we are going to be doing in this future Paradise upon earth we are not entirely sure. There will be up to half the population of the World still living at the end of the seven year period of wrath. When it says the Lord is going to reign with a rod of iron, it is obvious some people are going to need real justice. I believe we will be helping to administer justice here on earth. Also, we will be busy putting the World back in order after the ruin caused during the holocaust. In Paul's epistle to the Corinthians he states, **Eye has not seen, nor ear heard; neither has it entered into the heart of man, the things that God has prepared for those who love him.**

So whatever God has lined up for us in the glorious one thousand year period has got to be better than we could ever imagine. There will be no hunger, no war nor need for weapons. Animals will not kill each other for meat, but rather the lamb will lie down with the wolf. The lion will eat grass like the ox. People will plant their own crops and enjoy the fruits of their labour without worrying about plagues or disease. No more hustle and bustle of modern day living or hassle over bills and debts. No more of the chaos and uncertainty and evil that pervades every street in every country of the World today.

What fun lies ahead for those of us who believe and await His return with patience. Only those whose names are written in the Book of Life will enjoy this future Paradise. Very few are chosen by the grace of God. Make sure your name is included so that you too can enjoy life eternal with God and His Son.

The desert and the parched land will be glad; the wilderness will rejoice and blossom. Like the crocus, it will burst into bloom; it will rejoice greatly and shout for joy. The glory of Lebanon will be given to it, the splendour of Carmel and Sharon; they will see the glory of the Lord, the splendour of our God. Strengthen the feeble hands, steady the knees that give way; say to those with fearful hearts, "Be strong, do not fear; your God will come, he will come with vengeance; with divine retribution he will come to save you." Then will the eyes of the blind be opened and the ears of the deaf unstopped. Then will the lame leap like a deer, and the mute tongue shout for joy. Water will gush forth in the wilderness and streams in the desert. The burning sand will become a pool, the thirsty ground bubbling springs. In the haunts where jackals once lay, grass and reeds and papyrus will grow. And a highway will be there; it will be called the Way of Holiness. The unclean will not journey on it; it will be for those who walk in that Way; wicked fools will not go about on it. No lion will be there, nor will any ferocious beast get up on it; they will not be found there. But only the redeemed will walk there, and the ransomed of the Lord will return. They will enter Zion with singing; everlasting joy will overtake them, and sorrow and sighing will flee away. (Isaiah 35:1-10)

chapter 11
WHERE IS JESUS CHRIST NOW?

Before I became a believer, the name Jesus Christ was just a swear word to me. It never occurred to me that this man actually existed, walked on the earth and did normal things. I never realised that our calendar was based on the year of his birth. It was just religion to me. Yet Josephus, a noted Jewish historian and a non-Christian, actually recorded the resurrection in Jewish history.

It was word of mouth for the most part, and word of his deeds spread like wild-fire. Therefore when He actually rose from the dead and appeared to people (over five hundred people on one particular occasion), it had huge repercussions. After the Holy Spirit was poured out on the day of Pentecost, Peter preached with such boldness and power that about three thousand people believed, all at the same time. Peter was not a learned man, he was a fisherman—a peasant. He was endued with such power on the day the Holy Spirit was given that he rocked the very foundations of Judaism that day. Since then, beginning with the twelve apostles, Christian believers turned the World upside down and changed the course of history.

In Acts 1:10 on the Mount of Olives, Jesus Christ gave last minute instructions to his apostles. After this He ascended up before their very eyes and a cloud hid Him from them. Then two men, dressed in white, stood beside them and said: *Ye men of Galilee why do you stand here looking into the sky? This same Jesus, who has been taken from you into heaven, will come back in the same way you have seen him go into heaven.*

So, where did Jesus Christ go? In John 14:3 Jesus said to his disciples, In my Father's house there are many mansions. I go to prepare a place for you, and if I go and prepare a place for you I will come back and take you to be with me, that you also may be where I am.

In Hebrews it says He passed through the heavens. Therefore, He is out there somewhere getting a place ready for us. When we meet Him in the clouds with all the other saints, He will take us to this destination for the duration of the Great Tribulation. At the end of the tribulation, when Jesus comes back to the Mount of Olives, we are coming back with him. This time He is coming back as a military power and not as a servant. He is returning to the Mount of Olives just as the two messengers said He would, and He is coming with his saints in great power and glory.

Very often today, programs on TV and articles in newspapers debate the question "Is there life on other planets?" Commentators often conclude, from a mathematical and logical point of view, that because there are many billions of planets and galaxies, there must be other life forms out there somewhere in the universe. We are even sending out radio messages into space in the hope that some other intelligence might respond in kind. Well, I have news for all those wondering if there is anybody else out there—there is!

Jesus Christ is not an angel. He is a man with extra spiritual dimensions. Remember He said to Thomas **I am not a ghost**. He is out there, sitting on the right hand of God, preparing a place for us. The Bible does describe this Heavenly City in chapter 21 of the Book of Revelation. (A fuller discussion of the Fallen Angels of Genesis 6, the Great Pyramid of Giza and the future City of God—the New Jerusalem—can be found in my book The Nephilim and the Pyramid of the Apocalypse.) But you can be sure that it is a location with food, air, water, etc. After all, Christ Jesus is a man so I presume He must eat, drink and breathe. God's work on this earth was a beautiful Paradise before Lucifer's fall from grace and subsequent interference. So we can be sure that the place we are going to when Jesus Christ returns is going to be beautiful also. I am looking forward to it.

Wherever "heaven" is, whether it is in another galaxy or another dimension, it is a "place." So when you hear people ask if there is life on other planets, the answer is "yes." Jesus Christ is there. God is there also, along with twenty-four elders. Throughout the Book of Revelation, it talks of twenty-four elders who are in heaven with God and with Jesus Christ and the angels. They are mentioned lots of times, but we are not told who they are or what their function is. So there is no point in guessing. There are also myriads of spirit beings called angels or messengers who are men but are spirit in nature. In Revelation 5 it says there are **ten thousand times ten thousand** angels surrounding the throne. And there are many more besides these. God is spirit also. I am sure this place is far away, but this is no problem to spirit beings, as they can transcend physical boundaries and move faster than the speed of light.

If man looked into the Bible for answers, rather than listening to psychics, mediums and spiritualists for answers, he or she would learn the truth, and the **truth will set you free** (John 8:32).

chapter 12
MESSANGERS

In the previous chapter, two men dressed in white, who spoke to the apostles on the Mount of Olives, were mentioned. These two men were probably Gabriel and Michael. These are spirit beings we call angels. The Greek word for angels is *aggelos*, meaning messenger or agent. Very often we think of angels as little cherubims resembling children in the nude with no genitalia that fly about with little wings. Other images are of fully-grown men or women with massive wings protruding from their backs. A study of these messengers in the Bible portrays a different picture. They are called men and many times they are not recognised as spirit beings but rather as ordinary men. For instance, God sent two angels into Sodom and Gomorrah to tell Lot and his family to leave. After they entered Lot's house, it says all the men of Sodom and Gomorrah went to Lot's house, shouting **send out those two men so that we can have sex with them** (Genesis 19:5). So angels obviously look like men. However, we are flesh and blood, but these spirit beings are not and are therefore not restricted to the same constraints as us mortals. The point is that there are millions of these spirit beings in heaven.

In Matthew 26:53 when the mob led by Judas came to arrest Jesus, He told them that He had over twelve legions of angels at his disposal if He needed them. A legion consisted of six thousand men. He had at his command seventy- two thousand of these spirit men if He needed them. By contrast it says in 2 Corinthians 11:14 that Satan himself masquerades as an **angel of light**. In Revelation 12 the Bible describes a war in heaven between Michael and his angels and the devil and his angels. Elsewhere it talks of the original rebellion in heaven between Lucifer, as he was then called, and God. Lucifer endeavoured to overthrow God, but he was defeated. The devil still has access to heaven, for we are told **that day and night he appears before God, accusing the brethren.** But in Revelation 12 he is defeated by Michael and is cast to earth, and his fallen angels are cast down with him. They are the invisible spirit beings that control and cause the evil that has been on earth ever since the fall of man. As Lucifer means **bearer of light**, he knows how to appear as an apostle of light. **And no wonder, for Satan himself masquerades as an angel of light. It is not surprising then, if his servants masquerade as servants of righteousness. Their end will be what their actions deserve** (2 Corinthians ll: 14-15).

So it is important for us to question anyone who purports to represent God and Jesus. If you cannot document truth, line by line and verse by verse from the Word of God, then you will be prone to error and will be deceived.

Jesus Christ in his risen body was the same Jesus the apostles knew before He was crucified, but He now had extra potential. He walked and talked with two of the disciples for eight miles, and they did not know who He was. Doubting Thomas said he would not believe Jesus Christ had risen from the dead until he saw the holes in his hands and touched the wound in his ribs. When Jesus subsequently met Thomas, He invited him to touch him and feel him saying I am not a ghost.

In John 21 it says Jesus ate fish with Peter and some of the other disciples. At the last supper He said He would not drink of the fruit of the vine until He was in Paradise with them in the future. Paradise is on earth, so although He had a new spiritual body, He was still the same man. I am looking forward to eating some fish and drinking some wine with him in Paradise.

When He returns to gather us together with him, we too will get a new spiritual body like his. I personally will be looking for a fresh head of hair and a new hip and perhaps a more streamlined physique!

Because angels are spirits, they can transcend physical constraints. The speed of light is 186,000 miles per second. People cannot travel at the speed of light because they are flesh and blood. However, spirit beings, both good and evil, can travel faster than the speed of light because the spirit is outside the physical constraints of flesh and blood. Therefore it is easy for angels to speed from their place in heaven to earth even if it is millions of light years away. For God is not constrained by time and space as we are. So, according to the Word of God, the Bible, there is life out there somewhere. Intelligent life exists out there—more intelligent than us. In this place called heaven in the Bible, lives the man Christ Jesus, with God and an innumerable amount of spirit beings known to us as angels.

chapter 13
ALPHA & OMEGA-FIRST & LAST

In olden times, military conflict was a constant reality. Kings would have watch-outs and soldiers along their borders to give them early warning should they come under invasion or attack. If an enemy army was approaching, a runner would be immediately dispatched to run to the nearest town to warn them that the enemy was at the border. If the enemy advanced further into their territory, another runner would speed back to the headquarters and tell them that the enemy was, say, fifty miles away. Then another scout would come and say they are forty miles away. This would give the occupants of the town enough time to take action. These runners would keep coming until finally the last one would run in and say "I am the Alpha and Omega, the first and the last, the enemy is only three miles away, get out of town quickly and run for your lives."

In Revelation 1:8 it says, **I am the Alpha and Omega.** At the end of the book of Revelation 22:13 it says the same thing and adds, **the beginning and the end, the first and the last.** This is Jesus Christ speaking. Alpha and Omega are the first and last letters of the Greek alphabet. He says He is the First and the Last, the Beginning and the End.

When Jesus Christ opens the Book of Revelation with **I am the Alpha and Omega**, He is giving us a clear warning. He is saying that the time is very short. These things are about to happen so we had better take the appropriate action or else face the consequences of our inaction. What more warning can God, via Jesus Christ, give us? Just as Noah warned his contemporaries of the impending flood and Moses warned the Egyptians of the plagues and the deaths of the firstborn, Jesus Christ is telling us here that the enemy is almost upon us. He is saying that the days ahead of us are going to be worse than those in Noah's day or any day since the beginning of this World. Do not make the same mistakes as those who have gone before. Put your trust in God and His son, Jesus Christ.

Behold I stand at the door and knock: If any man hear my voice and open the door, I will come in to him and will sup with him, and he with me. (Revelation 3:20)

It was the Oriental custom that if a visitor came to your house to eat, he or she sat and ate and you served him or her and looked after him or her, but you did not eat with your visitor. Jesus Christ goes beyond this Eastern custom, He wants to actually sit down and eat with you. This symbolises that He wants to be your intimate friend. He wants you to know him. People will often let you down and disappoint you, but Jesus Christ will never let you down.

Come unto me all ye that labour and are heavy laden, and I will give you rest. Take my yoke upon you and learn of me; for I am meek and lowly in heart: and you shall find rest unto your souls. (Matthew 11:28-29)

chapter 14

THE PASSOVER

Many things that happened in the Old Testament were metaphors for what would occur in the future. Take the Passover for instance. The children of Israel had been slaves to The Pharaoh for 430 years. God spoke to Moses and told him to go to The Pharaoh and ask him to **let my people go** or else various plagues would come upon them. The Pharaoh refused, and the plagues ensued. God then told Moses to tell The Pharaoh that if he did not let the children of Israel go, a terrible thing would befall them; the eldest male in every family would die. Also, the firstborn of all livestock would die. He also told the Israelites to ask the Egyptians for silver, gold and clothes. God told Moses that each household was to take a one year old lamb, without spot or blemish, kill the lamb and take the blood and put it over their doors and on the sides of the doors. Then they had to roast the lamb over a fire and eat it all (Exodus 12).

In the middle of the night, the firstborn son of every household in Egypt died, also the firstborn of all livestock. There was incredible wailing and sorrow throughout Egypt. Pharaoh finally told Moses to get out quickly. God called this the Passover, for He passed over every house that had the blood on the doors, and they were saved. So the children of Israel gained freedom from slavery and by eating the meat they received strength to journey to the Promised Land. This happened years before Christ was born. Every year they perform the Passover in memory of their release.

When John the Baptist saw Jesus Christ, the first thing he said was **behold the lamb of God who takes away the sin of the World.** Later, at the last supper, Jesus Christ took wine and shared it with His apostles. He said that this wine represented His blood, which was shed for the remission of sin. He then took bread and broke it saying **this is my body, which is broken for you.**

Jesus Christ was crucified and died at the very same time the Jews killed their Passover lamb. He spilled his blood on the cross for us to be saved. Before they crucified him, they beat him so badly that his face could not be recognised. He became our Passover Lamb. He was the acceptable sacrifice for man's redemption for He had no spot or blemish. He was innocent and because He was born of God, his blood was pure and clean. He did not deserve to die for He had no sin. So by the shedding of his blood He paid the price for man's redemption.

He became the lamb who takes away the sin of the World. When we believe Jesus Christ died for us we are cleansed of our sin and death will ultimately pass over us. Because His body was broken for us, He took our sickness upon himself so that not only do we have eternal life in the future but also physical strength to journey through the slavery of this life on our way to the Promised Land in the future.

He told his disciples that He would not drink wine until He

was with them in Paradise. That will be our ultimate destination. When we have a holy communion, and we sip the wine, it is to remind us of His blood, which has saved us from death. When we break the bread we are reminded of His body, which was broken for us. This is the significance of the communion. The Passover Lamb that God instructed Moses to implement all those years before Christ was a metaphor for Christ's death and our salvation.

chapter 15

THE WORD OF GOD

You have been called up for jury duty. They bring you into the court and show you the accused man. Then they ask you "is this man guilty or not guilty?" You say you don't know because you haven't heard the evidence. How can you make a judgement if you haven't heard the evidence? You can't. Well it is the same with those of us who were raised Roman Catholics. With regard to what the Bible says on many subjects, we have never been shown the evidence.

We received one inch of the truth of the Word of God and six miles of tradition and theology. We were never really taught the truths of God's Word as Roman Catholics, so, consequently, we do not believe it. You cannot believe in something of which you have no knowledge. From my over thirty years of studying God's Word and having discussed biblical matters with many priests, I have come to the conclusion that very few priests have any knowledge or real belief in the veracity of the Bible. Therefore, it is no wonder that they cannot communicate these truths to their parishioners; you cannot give someone the flu if you do not have it.

For many to call themselves Christians today is like someone telling you that they are a mechanic but don't know how to change the oil in your car. Yet it is so easy to scoff at people who say the Bible has the answers. Everywhere today true Christian believers are ridiculed and labeled Bible thumpers and fundamentalists and nutcases.

On radio and television it is fine to promote homosexuals, lesbians, transvestites, fortune tellers and other anti-Christian values.

However, these same promoters do not want anybody on air discussing the merits of the Word of God and Jesus Christ. This is no wonder to us who have discovered the truth, for it was always this way. All through the Old Testament, anytime a prophet or a man of God came with a message to tell, he invariably got his head lopped off by the political and religious establishment.

Who do you believe crucified Jesus Christ? I was taught at school that Pontius Pilate was to blame. However, I discovered later that he wanted to release Jesus, so he washed his hands of the decision. My Bible says the ones that set Jesus Christ up and had him tortured and murdered were the religious leaders of the day—the Chief Priests and the Pharisees. Today, it is religious leaders that label Christian groups as cults and sects. Historically Satan's realm of influence has always been the religious. He is the one who hates the truth of the Word of God because it exposes him and his work. As long as he can keep people away from the light of the truth and keep them counting beads and praying to statues, he is happy. We were always treated like mushrooms: Keep them in the dark and feed them manure. When people discover the truth as revealed in the Word of God, they realise who they are in Christ and what power they have as a result of what Jesus Christ accomplished.

When He was on earth He demonstrated the two opposing powers to people. He exposed the works of the devil on the one hand and demonstrated the love and goodness of the one true God on the other. He turned over the rock and showed people the snake that was hiding underneath it.

Today, for the most part, people don't believe in the devil. There is no sin, no good, no evil and no God. Today New Age religion is reliance on self. We are told that we have the power within ourselves to influence the future. There is no need for an Almighty God. Good and evil is within us and we have the power to be our own Gods. Well, the Bible teaches that there are two Gods. One is the true God and Father of the Lord Jesus Christ, and the other is called the "god of this World." He is also referred to as the Prince of this World, the Prince of Darkness and the Prince of the Power of the Air. Other names given to him are: the Serpent, the Deceiver, the Accuser, the Adversary, Lucifer, Baal and Beelzebub.

You may remember the account from Luke 4 when the devil took Jesus up into a high mountain and showed Him all the glories of the World in a moment of time—it takes a lot of power to do that. Then he said to Jesus Christ, **all this power [authority] will I give to you. For it is delivered unto me and to whomsoever I will, I give it.** How could he offer to give all this power to Jesus Christ, whom he knew was the Son of God, if he didn't have it? Well, he does have this power, for he got the dominion from Adam when he transgressed in the garden. Jesus Christ knew Satan had the power, but of course He did not fall for the bait.

Satan also said, **to whomsoever I will, I give it.** Now you know who gave Hitler the power. Also Stalin, Pol Pot, Saddam Hussein and so on. He will give it to you too if you want it, but you will pay the ultimate price.

The point is that many Catholics and so-called Christians have never been shown the evidence. We have never heard enough to be able to form a decision based on knowledge, since we have had very little biblical training. For the Word of God is a bit like a jigsaw puzzle. As you put the bits together, after a while you begin to see the picture. Then when you have seen enough of the picture you can determine what the picture says.

When I was a youth, our Mass was in Latin! Imagine Jesus Christ going out to teach the Word of God to ordinary people using a foreign language that nobody understood! It makes no sense. As a result we have a lot of older people who have faith that does not come from knowledge. Most of the younger generation does not believe in the Roman Catholic teaching because they can see the hypocrisy in it. With the recent revelations and scandals associated with the Church of Rome, it is hard to remain loyal.

This reminds me of a parable Jesus Christ told of one man who built his house upon the sand and the other who built his house upon the rock. When the storm and the floods arose the sands were washed away, and the first house perished. When the same storms beat upon the other house it survived because it was built upon a rock. Well, Jesus Christ is that rock.

We were told Peter was the first Pope—Christ's vicar on earth. **Thou art Peter and upon this rock I will build my church.** This is a great lie. In the original text, Peter's name in the Greek is "Petros" meaning a very small stone or a grain of sand. This is what this literally means. Peter adhered to the Word one day and didn't the next. One day he wanted to die for Jesus, and the next day he denied him and ran away and hid himself. **But upon this rock [Petra] I will build my church.** The Greek word petra means a big immovable rock. It is the total opposite of petros. We get the word petrified from this word. Jesus Christ was talking about himself when He said **I will build my church upon a rock.**

In many places in the Old Testament, God is referred to as our rock, and in the New Testament Jesus Christ is referred to as the rock upon which the church is built. He is also called the chief cornerstone. You cannot build a church upon an ordinary man like Peter. Yes, he was a great leader in the early Christian church, but he made mistakes. On a purely human level, the apostle Paul received much more revelation than Peter did, and he was not even one of the original twelve apostles.

Another lie that was taught and that has caused many to err is the teaching that Mary is the mother of God. Well she is not. God does not have a mother. Mary was a wonderful believer in God for she said, **be it unto me according to thy Word.** She is called **blessed** because she believed God and brought forth Jesus Christ, the lamb of God, who subsequently redeemed mankind.

Jesus, the Bible says, was her firstborn. So she must have had other children. In fact, if you read Matthew 13 it names her four sons and mentions that she had daughters as well:

> *Isn't this the carpenter's son? Isn't his mother's name Mary, and his brothers James, Joseph, Simon and Judas, aren't all his sisters with us? Where then did this man get all these things? And they took offence at him. (Matthew 13:55-57)*

It is universally accepted that Mary was a virgin when Jesus Christ was conceived by the Holy Spirit, but after Jesus was born she had a normal marriage relationship with her young husband Joseph, and they had other children.

Ever wonder why it's called the "Assumption of Mary into heaven"? It is because they "assumed" it happened—Mary is dead just like everyone else and is awaiting the return of her son from heaven to take her out just like Joseph, Matthew, Mark, Luke, John, Paul and all the other Christians who have lived and died since the time of Pentecost.

Consequently, praying to Mary for favours as the "Mother of God" is totally wrong. We are told that **there is one God and one mediator between man and God, the man Christ Jesus** (1 Timothy 2:5).

These are just a few examples of the lies we have been taught as Roman Catholics. I do not wish to target the Roman Catholic church alone. It is just that having been raised Roman Catholic I feel qualified to speak on it. But most of the so-called Christian churches are far removed from Jesus Christ and his teaching. It is not uncommon to hear of some Protestant Archbishop declare that he does not believe in the virgin birth or the resurrection. You can be a homosexual and still become a Methodist minister. All the mainstream churches have more in common with the Chief Priests and Pharisees than with the doctrine of the Bible.

All these religions are man-made. According to the Word of God, there are only three categories of people. In the Old Testament people were either Jew or Gentile. Then on the day of Pentecost, when the Holy Spirit was given for the first time, there was a third category known as Church of God. These are people, either Jewish or Gentile, who believe in the resurrection of Christ and thus receive the spirit of Christ in them. They then become members of the Church of God and part of the Body of Christ. He is the head and we are members of His body. So you are, biblically speaking, either a Jew, a Gentile or a real believer in Christ, making you a Christian. As was stated earlier, as long as Satan can keep people in the dark, keep them praying to idols of stone and wood, fill their minds with foolish doctrine and tradition, then he has succeeded in keeping them ignorant of the truth.

I am the light of the World as long as a man follows me, he shall not walk in darkness. (John 8:12)

If you are walking in the pitch dark, then you are stumbling around. You cannot see what is in front of you or what is behind you. The next step you take you may fall into a hole. But when you discover Jesus Christ, when you realise who He is and what He has accomplished by his death and resurrection, then you receive light. When you have the light, then you can walk through the darkness with confidence. If you come to a hole, you can step around it. You can see what is in front of you and what is behind you and what is beside you because you have the light, and all the darkness in the World cannot put out that light.

In the book of Isaiah written years before Christ, the prophecy said that the true Messiah would open the eyes a man who was born blind. In the Gospel of John chapter 9, Jesus Christ fulfills this prophecy written all those years before. This man was born in the dark so to speak. All his life he wandered around not seeing where he was going. When he received his sight from Jesus Christ then he could see all those things that he could only imagine before. If he had ten other blind friends whom he grew up with, and he went to them and said "I can see," his friends could say "no you can't see; we don't believe you can see," and that is their prerogative.

Sometimes I feel we believers are like this blind man. Most

of our lives we were in the dark. Then, by the grace of God, we learned about Jesus Christ and found the knowledge of God in the Word. Our eyes were opened, and we got the gift of The Holy Spirit and with it the promise of eternal life. When we tried to tell our friends about it, many of them did not believe us. They did not want to know. We wanted to take them by the hand and show them the way, but they refused to be shown.

When millions of true Christians mysteriously disappear, those of you who remain will still have the chance to turn to Jesus Christ and accept him as your Saviour. This choice may mean a hard and perilous time ahead for you, but if you endure, salvation will be your ultimate reward. If you choose not to believe, then you will remain in darkness forever and will perish.

Is it not obvious that as Roman Catholics we were ignorant of the teachings of the Bible as so much of it contradicts directly what we were taught? The following statement from Jesus Christ is another illustration of how we were kept in the dark:

> And do not call anyone on earth "Father," for you have one Father, and He is in heaven. (Matthew 23:9)

The Roman Catholic church is beginning to crumble. Fewer young people are finding vocations, and the present clergy are getting older. Young people do not believe because they see it as a dead, empty exercise.

The flood of scandals that have affected the Catholic Church in recent years has seen it attacked from every quarter. Even older lay people feel cheated and betrayed. The reason the church is falling is because it is built upon sand (Petros). The only church that can and will prevail is the Church of God that is built upon the solid rock

(Petra) of Jesus Christ with the Word of God as its sure foundation. All other religions are destined to fail because they are built upon the sand of tradition and the laws of men.

chapter 16

TRUTH VS. TRADITION

God is very jealous of His Word. By that I mean, He expects Christians to know His truth and to live by its precepts. He hates untruths and lies. If we are to walk in His ways, it behooves us to know the truth. The truth can only be found in the Word of God, the Bible. Many people have a wishy-washy, blasé attitude towards how they think God wants to be worshipped. This is how we were taught all our lives, so it must be OK with God, they think. Well, this is the wrong attitude. For example, much of what we were taught as Roman Catholics is mere tradition. It is very often totally opposite to the written and revealed Word of God. Let us see what Jesus Christ had to say about "tradition."

Then some Pharisees and teachers of the law came to Jesus from Jerusalem and asked, "Why do your disciples break the tradition of the elders? They don't wash their hands before they eat." Jesus replied, "And why do you break the command of God for the sake of your tradition?...You hypocrites! Isaiah was right when he prophesied about you: 'These people honour me with their lips, but their hearts are far from me. They wor-

ship me in vain; their teachings are but rules taught by men.'"
(Matthew 15:1-3, 7-9)

The Scribes and Pharisees were the religious rulers and leaders of their day. Today, they would be the Priests and Bishops, Vicars, Ayatollahs, Rabbis, etc. In Jesus' time there were all sorts of traditions, such as you had to wash your hands before eating or else you were breaking one of their man-made commandments. God had no such commandment. Another was that all mirrors had to be taken off the walls on the Sabbath. God had commanded that no work be done on the Sabbath. Therefore, the religious rulers decided that if a woman was walking past a mirror on the Sabbath and she saw a grey hair and pulled it out, that would be breaking the commandment!

There are hundreds of traditions in the Roman Catholic church. In fact almost all of the dogma and doctrine is based on commandments of men and very little attention is paid to the Word of God. You will notice in the passage above that Jesus said, **you have made the Word of God of no effect because of your traditions.** The traditions have become doctrine and the Word of God remains a dusty old book that is paid lip service to by religious leaders. Nothing has changed in two thousand years. Satan is tricking people in the same old way he has always done. The religious of our day are playing right into his hands.

To illustrate how important to God the accuracy of His Word is, let us look at another short passage from Matthew 16:

From that time on Jesus began to explain to his disciples that he must go to Jerusalem and suffer many things at the hands of the elders, chief priests and teachers of the

law, and that he must be killed and on the third day be
raised to life. Peter took him aside and began to rebuke
him. "Never, Lord!" he said. "This shall never happen
to you!" (Matthew 16:21-22)

Jesus Christ was the Son of God. He knew what He had come
to do and what needed to be accomplished. He was in direct communication with God, His Father. Everything He said and did was
planned since before the foundations of the World (Ephesians 1:4).
In this instance, He is telling his disciples what is about to become
of Him. He is speaking the Word of God to them; He is speaking
the truth. Peter is a hard man, nobody is going to mess with the boss
while Peter is around. He'll see to that!! What does Jesus reply?

Jesus turned and said to Peter, "Get behind me Satan! You are
a stumbling block [snare] to me; you do not have in mind the
things of God but the things of men." (Matthew 16:23)

This is the same Peter that we were told was the first Pope.
They never told us this verse though. You see, Peter was an action
man, always ready to jump in. But very often when he opened his
mouth, he put both feet in it. Jesus Christ was the Word of God,
and he was speaking the truth. When you go away from the Word
of God, then you are in error. The Word of God is a narrow path.
When you stray from the path, you are in the spiritual wilderness.

The Word of God is the light of the World. Any man who
walks in Jesus Christ has the light and can see where he is going.
But when you go away from the light, then you are in the darkness
again. And God is not pleased when we do not follow the Word of
God, especially when we know what the truth is and choose to do
the opposite.

Peter was very close to Jesus. He was his right-hand man in many ways and was a natural leader. They had been through many things together and were good friends. Yet Jesus Christ turned around, looked Peter straight in the eye and said **Get thee behind me Satan**. I bet that shook Peter up a bit. He rebuked him in front of all his peers. Peter was man enough to swallow his medicine and get on with it. In another situation, regarding money, Jesus rebuked Judas Iscariot. However, rather than learn from his chastening, Judas, smarting after the rebuke, went off and betrayed Jesus to the authorities and the mob.

So there you have the difference between truth and tradition. There has been a mountain of tradition taught and preached in the name of Christianity all over the World in the past two thousand years. Millions have died in so called "holy" wars and other millions murdered in attempting to convert natives to this so-called Christianity. During the Spanish Inquisition millions died because they refused to believe the traditions of the Church of Rome.

chapter 17

WHO AND WHAT ARE "THE SAINTS"?

An epistle is an old-fashioned name for what we call a letter. The apostle Paul wrote several epistles or letters. This was in the early days of the apostles, when Christianity was very dynamic and when signs, miracles and wonders abounded wherever the Word of God was preached. As many people converted with the news of the resurrection of Jesus Christ, the Church grew and spread. Many disciples, including Paul, traveled far and wide in the then known World, teaching people about Christ and establishing communities of believers known as "churches."

The word church comes from the Greek word *eklesia* meaning *called out*. So, in its original meaning in the Bible, the word church does not mean a building or an edifice of some description but rather a group of people who have been called out from the rest of the people.

By the same token, the Greek word for saint is *hagios*, meaning *set apart, separate* or *holy*. In our culture, and according to religious tradition, a saint is someone whose profound holiness is formally recognised after death by a recognised Christian Church. This is not the definition of a saint according to the Word of God.

A saint is merely a person who has accepted Jesus Christ as his or her personal Saviour and who believes that God raised him from the dead (Romans 10:9-10). When an individual believes this in the depths of his or her heart, he or she receives the Spirit of God and is saved. Every person who believes in Christ is a saint: a person who has been set apart from those who do not believe. If one believes in Christ, this makes one holy in so far as he or she is now the child of God with eternal life. This person is going to heaven because he or she believes in what Christ has done for him or her, and all hell cannot stop this individual from getting there.

There are seven epistles specifically addressed to and concerning the Church of God. These epistles or letters were written by Paul but authored by God. All of these epistles begin with who they are written to and their address: Paul to the Church in Rome, who are loved of God and called to be saints, (Romans 1:1,7); Paul unto the Church of God, which is at Corinth, called to be saints (1 Corinthians 1:2); Paul unto the Church of God, which is at Corinth, with all the saints that are in all Achaia (1 Corinthians 1:1) and Paul, an apostle of Jesus Christ by the will of God, to the saints that are at Ephesus (Ephesians 1:1).

All of these seven epistles or letters are addressed to the saints at Rome, Corinth, Ephesus, Galatia, Phillipe, Collasse and Thessalonica. In our terms today, they would be addressed to the "called out" of God—the "separated" or "set apart" people who have believed. Thus everyone who believes is a saint according to God's Word. My name is Patrick so I presume I am a "Saint Patrick"! There were saints in the Old Testament, there are saints in our present day, and there will be saints in the days of the Great Tribulation (Revelation ll:18,13:7).

Multitudes of people will turn to the one true God and to His Son in the post-Rapture period called the tribulation. Many of these saints will die because of their faith in this period. Ultimately everyone who believes in the Lord Jesus Christ will be saved and will one day soon, see Him face to face.

chapter 18
AMERICA AND EUROPE IN PROPHECY

Nebuchadnezzar was the king and ruler of the Babylonian Empire about 2,500 years ago. The prophet Daniel had risen to a position of authority in Nebuchadnezzar's government because of his knowledge and learning. He and the Jewish nation were in captivity in the Babylonian Empire at that time.

The king had a dream one night that greatly troubled him. He called for his advisers to interpret this dream. He would not tell them what the dream was because he did not want them to fabricate an interpretation. They had to tell him what the dream was and then give the meaning of it.

His advisers, magicians, sorcerers and astrologers could not tell him what his dream was, let alone give him the meaning of it. At this, Nebuchadnezzar was very upset and ordered all the wise men of Babylon to be executed. Daniel stepped in and offered the emperor an alternative solution. He said that if he could tell the king his dream and give him the meaning of it, then the lives of all the wise men of Babylon should be spared. The king agreed.

Daniel prayed to God for the details of the dream and the interpretation. He then went to Nebuchadnezzar and told him that only God can reveal mysteries of things to come and give interpretations of dreams.

> *You looked, O King, and there before you stood a large statue—an enormous, dazzling statue, awesome in appearance. The head of the statue was made of pure gold, its chest and arms of silver, its belly and thighs of bronze, its legs of iron, its feet partly in iron and partly of baked clay. While you were watching, a rock was cut out, but not by human hands. It struck the statue on its feet of iron and clay and smashed them. Then the iron, the clay, the bronze, the silver and the gold were broken to pieces at the same time and became like chaff on the threshing floor in summer. The wind swept them away without leaving a trace. But the rock that struck the statue became a huge mountain and filled the whole earth. (Daniel 2:31-35)*

The king was amazed at the accuracy of the detail of his dream. Daniel then went on to give the interpretation of the statue the king had seen and the meaning thereof.

Daniel told the king that the four parts of the statue represented four mighty kingdoms that would rule the World. The first kingdom was the Babylonian Empire and Nebuchadnezzar was the first ruler—**You are the head of gold**. Daniel then went on to explain that the other three parts were kingdoms that would rule the World in future years. The arms of silver represented the Medo-Persian Empire that conquered Babylon only a few years later. The thighs of bronze represented the Greek Empire , which subsequently controlled most of the then known World under Alexander the Great.

Finally, Daniel describes a fourth kingdom in verses 40-44. This prophecy is only partially fulfilled and therefore awaits complete fulfillment. This fourth kingdom was believed to be the Roman Empire. The iron heel of Rome ruled for many centuries until it collapsed because of decadence. Daniel spoke of the statue having feet with ten toes made of iron mixed with clay, and he said that a huge rock would finally smash the feet and turn the whole statue to dust. This rock is of course Jesus Christ. When He returns He will establish His Kingdom where God's will will be done on earth as it is in heaven. I used to believe that the European Union was this future government that would be ruled over by the Antichrist, but I do not now believe this to be the case.

A careful examination of the prophecies relating to this future government specifically state that it will be a global confederacy. It will not be confined to one geographic area, but rather it will be a club of ten members ruled by ten kings. At present we have a club of powerful economic interests called the G-8. But this future union will be global and will be grouped into a ten member society. Each of these ten members will be ruled over by ten "kings" who will be ruled over by the Antichrist. I have no doubt that Europe and the USA will play prominent roles in these future alignments. In fact, I believe that it will be a huge military and political alliance from the West that is destined to meet the 200 million strong army from the East in the final showdown at Armageddon.

Many commentators say that the United States of America is not mentioned in End Times prophecy. But if , as some say, this future global union is partly made up of the old Roman Empire revived, then the US will be part of it. If we look at the origin of the ethnic groups of people that make up the citizens of the US, the vast majority of them come from Europe, which formed the basis of the old Roman Empire. (For an in-depth study of the "feet of iron mixed with clay," and what exactly will occur when the Fallen Angels reappear during the Apocalypse, see the article entitled *Revelation Rapture* by this author published November 2006 in the online magazine *OFFICIAL DISCLOSURE*, which can be accessed at www.raidersnewsupdate.com).

Now look at another vision received by Daniel in chapter 7. Here he sees the same four kingdoms, but this time they are called "beasts." The last beast is this future global union, which is described as mighty and powerful, devouring everything in its march. Now observe the following prophecy:

> *The ten horns are ten kings who will come from this kingdom. After them another king will arise, differing from the earlier ones; he will subdue three kings. He will speak against the Most High and oppress his saints and try to change the set times and the laws. The saints will be handed over to him for a time, times and half a time. (Daniel 7:24-25)*

Here we have a confederacy of ten members. There may be several countries combined together in each association. The Antichrist will put down three "kings" and will persecute the saints and speak blasphemy against the Most High. This is corroborated in 2 Thessalonians 2:3-4 and in Revelation 17:12-13.

> *The ten horns you saw are ten kings who have not yet received a kingdom, but who for one hour will receive authority as kings along with the beast. They have one purpose and will give their power and authority to the beast.*

This prophecy says that in the tribulation period, a ten "kingdom" confederacy will emerge. These ten kingdoms will give authority and power to the beast who is the Antichrist. This ten kingdom confederacy is a One World government that will be established with the Antichrist as its leader. A pseudo peace will then begin on earth, and everyone will believe that this new great leader will be the one to solve all the problems of the World. For a time, peace will reign, and all the peoples of the earth will enjoy the good life. But about half way through the seven years, all hell will begin to break loose.

When the great nation from the North together with other Arab nations attack Israel, they will be defeated utterly with fire and brimstone by God. The massacre will be so great that it will take seven months to bury the dead (Ezekiel 39:12). Sifting through Scripture, it is evident that this power from the north is Russia. The devastation wrought on them and their Arab allies will be so great that it will create a huge political and military vacuum in the Middle East.

The Antichrist will seize the opportunity to move into the region. If this is the leader of an economically and militarily powerful Western Union, it is quite feasible that the United States of America will be involved. We know from recent history that the US with Europe moved speedily into the Gulf war, and then the US with Britain and some other countries went into Iraq. These countries' reasoning to move into war speedily again will be obvious: to protect their oil supply, which is vital to the industry of the whole of the Western Hemisphere.

With the demise of the military might of Russia and many of the Arab countries in the Middle East, it will be easy pickings for the Western powers to move into this region. Then the Antichrist will go into the Temple of God and proclaim that he is the true God and rightful world leader. About this time the "Kings of the East" begin to come into play and set their eyes eastward towards Palestine.

An army numbering 200 million will devastate millions as it begins to cut a swath westward. Up to a third of the population of the world will be wiped out as this great force exerts its power. The scene will then be set for a great confrontation between two of the greatest armies the world has ever witnessed. The battle will begin at the valley of Megiddo. This battle is called Armageddon.

We know that these prophecies are still future for two reasons. First, we are told that they will happen in **latter years**. Second, these events have never occurred before in history.

Over 2500 years ago Daniel prophesied that a rock, not cut by human hands, would smash the feet of the statue made from clay and iron. This is an obvious reference to the Lord Jesus Christ when He returns to the Mount of Olives. He is coming as a military ruler with his army of saints. Again the power of God will utterly rout the armies that oppose Him. Then He will begin to establish His Kingdom, which will last forever.

Do you remember the story of Joseph and the multicoloured dream coat? In it the Pharaoh had a dream where seven fat cows were devoured by seven thin cows. No one could interpret his dream until Joseph, another prophet of God, told him what the dream meant.

He told Pharaoh that they would have seven years of plenty followed by seven years of famine. Pharaoh was so impressed with Joseph that he put him in charge of the economy so that they would have enough food to see them through the famine years.

Can we not learn from this reality, which history bears out? If you are reading this after the disappearance of millions of Christians, then you are witnessing the fulfillment of prophecy. Provision must be made for the ensuing years of famine and scarcity of water that will ravage the world. The people who turn to God and Jesus Christ for refuge during the Great Tribulation are going to experience terrible hardship and persecution. As long as we know what lies ahead, we have the opportunity to do something about it.

In this respect, I want this book to give hope for the future. If you read this and the Rapture has not yet happened, then it offers you the chance to avoid the dreadful wrath that shall be visited upon this earth (see John 3:16, Roman 10:9-10).

If, however, the Rapture has occurred, then you must take action to provide as best you can for the terrifying days that are ahead. Trust in God and in His son the Lord Jesus Christ and your eternal future will be secured.

EPILOGUE

If you have read this book and the Rapture has not happened, you might want to know more. There is an abundance of material available in Christian book shops pertaining to prophecy and the Book of Revelation. Also you can obtain a Bible (the *New International Version* is recommended) and just start reading. I would suggest you begin at Matthew 1 and go from there. Always ask God to enlighten you, and He will. Remember:

> *Ask, and it shall be given you; seek and you shall find; knock, and it shall be opened unto you. (Matthew 7:7)*

If you are reading this book and millions of people have vanished from the earth, then all is not lost. God is still in business and He will not fail you. We are including the Book of Revelation and some other pertinent chapters in this book. If you can obtain a Bible then do so, and start reading and praying. There will be famine in the tribulation period. There will also be no water to drink in many areas of the world. I believe there will also be a collapse of the financial structures and markets worldwide. Therefore it would be wise to plant food and ensure you have a fresh, clean water supply. If you are reading this and the Rapture has not happened, then you might want to take steps to ensure that you will have food to eat and water to drink in the future.

I hope and pray that God blesses you as you read. If I have made any mistakes in the writing, then may God forgive me.

Appendix A
The Apocalypse: A Poem

On 26 February 1997, I was sitting in my car on Wellington Quay, Dublin. Having studied the material for this book for so long, I suddenly felt that I needed to write it all down in a poem. Although unprepared and rather busy, I decided to have a go. The following poem is the result. It is a summary of the events in the Book of Revelation and is biblically accurate. As these events are still future, I suppose it is a poem of prophecy. I wrote it in about an hour and ten minutes.

The Apocalypse

I

Upon the Isle of Patmos
In prayer on the Lord's day
The Spirit took me speedily
To an era far away.

II

He showed me things in visions
Which no man can see
Of days to come in future
Which verily shall be.

III

This day is nigh upon us
I feel convinced to say
Be ready or be warned
Man's sin the earth shall pay.

IV

The Raptured church shall usher in
A time before unknown
The man of sin shall take control
The World shall follow him.

V

With subtle words
And sleight of hand
And lies that shall deceive
Upon their heads, the mark to take
That brings them to the grave.

VI

The saints shall stand
Upon that day
His Word to uphold
Their blood will spill
She'll drink her fill
But in the end, be told.

VII

For they shall be rewarded
Who bend but do not break
To kiss the ring of Satan's Son
But trust in God's namesake.

VIII

Blood and fire and famine
Clouds black and noisome too
Death will stalk the living
The plague will prey on you.

IX

The Antichrist will rule the World
His will to bow the knee
His priest who sits upon the hills
Will blind their eyes to see.

X

The multitudes who throng the globe
In tumult 'ere shall be
The seas shall roar
The Beast will soar
Devouring bond and free.

XI

Black smoke of torment
Nere shall cease
For those who take the mark
The worm of death
Shall gnaw away
In death's bile grave so bleak.

XII

Eternally to gnash and wail
Because they choose the lie
And heeded not the Master's Son
Who gave His soul to die.

XIII

That we should be forgiven
Who trusted in the Word
Chosen from the beginning
To be our God's reward.

XIV

His first fruits from the dead are we
Who listened to His call
His voice our ear remembered
Predestined far beyond the fall
To walk in peace by waters still
In Paradise our hearts to fill
With pleasures glorious and thrill
Which eyes have never seen or heard
With Jesus Christ Our Lord's Shepherd.

XV

Some martyrs in that day shall fall
The saints with patience must endure
Who wrestle with the deathly pall
Of Satan's minnions, stink, vile, impure
Who hunt them down and kill the free
Refuse the mark, don't bend the knee
For in the end you'll see the light
Of God's abundant love and grace
And riches reap and know delight
And see your Saviour face to face.

XVI

The time is near
The angels wait
To put the sickle to the test
To reap the harvest of our God
To take the good, And leave the rest
To burn upon life's shallow grave

In terrible and fervent heat
The remnant of devil's chaff
The evidence of sin's defeat.

XVII

Beware you scornful and be warned
For soon the Rapture will befall
To catch away the faithful few
Who heard his voice, who got reborn
Who'll miss the wrath of the fearful day
Who'll live forever. Wait and pray.
Even so. Come quickly Lord Jesus.

Patrick Heron

Appendix B

Genesis Finds Its Complement in Revelation

References from the Book of Genesis	*References from the Book of Revelation*
Genesis, the book of the beginning	Apocalypse, the book of the end
The Earth created (1:1)	The Earth passed away (21:1)
Satan's first rebellion	Satan's final rebellion (20:3, 7-10)
Sun, moon and stars for Earth's with government (1:14-16)	Sun, moon, and stars, connected Earth's judgement (6:13, 8:12, 16:8)
Sun to govern the day (1:16)	No need of the sun (21:23)
Darkness called night (1:5)	No night there (22:5)
Waters called seas (1:10)	No more sea (21:1)
A river for Earth's blessing (2:10-14)	A river for the New Earth (22:1, 2)
Man in God's image (1:26)	Man headed by one in Satan's image (13)
Entrance of sin (3)	Development and end of sin (21, 22)
Curse pronounced (3:14, 17)	No more curse (22:3)
Death entered (3:19)	No more death (21:4)
Cherubim, first mentioned in connection with man (3:24)	Cherubim, finally mentioned in connection with man (4:6)
Man driven out from Eden (3:24)	Man restored (22)

References from the Book of Genesis	*References from the Book of Revelation*
Tree of life guarded (3:24)	Right to the Tree of Life (22:14)
Sorrow and suffering enter (3:17)	No more sorrow (21:4)
Man's religion, art and science, resorted to for enjoyment apart from God (4)	Man's religion, luxury, art and science, in their full glory, judged and destroyed by God (18)
Nimrod, a great rebel and king, and hidden anti-God, the founder of	The Beast, the great rebel, a king, a manifested anti-God, the reviver

Babylon (10: 8, 9)

A flood from God to destroy
an evil generation (6:9)

The Bow, the token of God's
covenant with the Earth (9:13)

Sodom and Egypt, the place of
corruption and temptation (13:19)

A confederacy against Abraham's
people overthrown (14)

Marriage of first Adam (2:18-23)

A bride sought for Abraham's son
(Isaac) is found (24)

Two angels acting for God on
behalf of His people (19)
on behalf of His people (11)

The promised seed coming into his
possession (11:18)

References from the
Book of Genesis

Man's dominion ceased and Satan's
begun (3:24)

The old serpent causing sin, suffering
and death (3:1)

The doom of the old serpent
pronounced (3:15)

Sun, moon and stars, associated
with Israel (37:9)

of Babylon (13:18)

A flood from Satan to destroy
an elect generation (12)

The Bow, betokening God's
remembrance of His covenant with
the Earth (4:3, 10:1)

Sodom and Egypt again (spiritually
representing Jerusalem) (11:8)

A confederacy against Abraham's
seed overthrown (12)

Marriage of last Adam (19)

A bride made ready and brought
to Abraham's Son (19:9)
See Matt 1:1

Two witnesses acting for God

A promised seed to possess the
gate of enemies (22:17)

References from the
Book of Revelation

Satan's dominion ended and
man's restored (22)

The old serpent bound for
1,000 years (20:1-3)

The doom of the old serpent
executed (20:10)

Sun, moon and stars again associated
with Israel (12)

Source: The Companion Bible (1974) London: EW Bullinger, Samuel Bagster and Sons Ltd

Appendix C
Gospel of Matthew

Chapter 24

¹ Jesus left the temple and was walking away when his disciples came up to him to call his attention to its buildings. ² "Do you see all these things?" he asked. "I tell you the truth, not one stone here will be left on another; every one will be thrown down." ³ As Jesus was sitting on the Mount of Olives, the disciples came to him privately. "Tell us," they said, "when will this happen, and what will be the sign of your coming and of the end of the age?" ⁴ Jesus answered: "Watch out that no one deceives you. ⁵ "For many will come in my name, claiming, 'I am the Christ,' and will deceive many. ⁶ "You will hear of wars and rumours of wars, but see to it that you are not alarmed. Such things must happen, but the end is still to come. ⁷ "Nation will rise against nation, and kingdom against kingdom. There will be famines and earthquakes in various places. ⁸ "All these are the beginning of birth pains. ⁹ "Then you will be handed over to be persecuted and put to death, and you will be hated by all nations because of me. ¹⁰ "At that time many will turn away from the faith and will betray and hate each other, ¹¹ "and many false prophets will appear and deceive many people. ¹² "Because of the increase of wickedness, the love of most will grow cold, ¹³ "but he who stands firm to the end will be saved. ¹⁴ "And this gospel of the kingdom will be preached in the whole world as a testimony to all nations, and then the end will come. ¹⁵ "So when you see standing in the holy place 'the abomination that causes desolation,' spoken of through the prophet Daniel—let the reader understand— ¹⁶ "then let those who are in Judea flee to

the mountains. [17] "Let no one on the roof of his house go down to take anything out of the house. [18] "Let no one in the field go back to get his cloak. [19] "How dreadful it will be in those days for pregnant women and nursing mothers! [20] "Pray that your flight will not take place in winter or on the Sabbath. [21] "For then there will be great distress, unequaled from the beginning of the world until now—and never to be equaled again. [22] "If those days had not been cut short, no one would survive, but for the sake of the elect those days will be shortened. [23] "At that time if anyone says to you, 'Look, here is the Christ!' or, 'There he is!' do not believe it. [24] "For false Christs and false prophets will appear and perform great signs and miracles to deceive even the elect—if that were possible. [25] "See, I have told you ahead of time. [26] "So if anyone tells you, 'There he is, out in the desert,' do not go out; or, 'Here he is, in the inner rooms,' do not believe it. [27] "For as lightning that comes from the east is visible even in the west, so will be the coming of the Son of Man. [28] "Wherever there is a carcass, there the vultures will gather. [29] "Immediately after the distress of those days 'the sun will be darkened, / and the moon will not give its light; / the stars will fall from the sky, / and the heavenly bodies will be shaken.' [30] "At that time the sign of the Son of Man will appear in the sky, and all the nations of the earth will mourn. They will see the Son of Man coming on the clouds of the sky, with power and great glory. [31] "And he will send his angels with a loud trumpet call, and they will gather his elect from the four winds, from one end of the heavens to the other. [32] "Now learn this lesson from the fig tree: As soon as its twigs get tender and its leaves come out, you know that summer is near. [33] "Even so, when you see all these things, you know that it is near, right at the door. [34] "I tell you the truth, this generation will certainly not pass away until all these things have happened. [35] "Heaven and earth will pass away, but my words will never pass away. [36] "No one knows about that day or hour, not even the angels in heaven, nor the Son, but only the Father. [37] "As it was in the days of Noah, so it will be at the coming of the Son of Man. [38] "For in the days before the flood, people were eating and drinking, marrying and giving in marriage, up to the day Noah entered the ark; [39] "and they knew nothing about what would happen until the flood came and took them all away. That is how it will be at the coming of the Son of Man. [40] "Two men will be in the field; one will be taken and the other left. [41] "Two women will be grinding with a hand mill; one will be taken and the other left. [42] "Therefore keep watch, because you do not know on what day your Lord will come. [43] "But understand this: If the owner of the house had known at what time of night the thief was coming, he would have kept watch and would not have let his house be broken into. [44] "So you also must be ready, because the Son of Man will come at an hour when you do not expect him. [45] "Who then is the faithful and wise servant, whom the master has put in charge of the servants in his household to give them their food at the proper time? [46] "It will be good for that servant whose master finds him doing so when he returns. [47] "I tell you the truth, he will put him in charge of all his possessions. [48] "But suppose that servant is wicked and says to himself, 'My master is staying away a long time,' [49] "and he then begins to beat his fellow-servants and to eat and drink with drunkards. [50] "The master of that servant will come on a day when he does not expect him and at an hour he is not aware of. [51] "He will cut him to pieces and assign him a place with the hypocrites, where there will be weeping and gnashing of teeth.

Book of Ezekiel
Written between 463–484 BC

Chapter 37

THE VALLEY OF DRY BONES

¹ The hand of the Lord was upon me, and he brought me out by the Spirit of the Lord and set me in the middle of a valley; it was full of bones. ² He led me back and forth among them, and I saw a great many bones on the floor of the valley, bones that were very dry. ³ He asked me, "Son of man, can these bones live?" I said, "O Sovereign Lord, you alone know." ⁴ Then he said to me, "Prophesy to these bones and say to them, 'Dry bones, hear the word of the Lord! ⁵ "'This is what the Sovereign Lord says to these bones: I will make breath enter you, and you will come to life. ⁶ "'I will attach tendons to you and make flesh come upon you and over you with skin, I will put breath in you, and you will come to life. Then you will know that I am the Lord.'" ⁷ So I prophesied as I was commanded. And as I was prophesying, there was a noise, a rattling sound, and the bones came together, bone to bone. ⁸ I looked, and tendons and flesh appeared on them and skin covered them, but there was no breath in them. ⁹ Then he said to me, "Prophesy to the breath; prophesy, son of man, and say to it, 'This is what the Sovereign Lord says: come from the four winds, O breath and breathe into these slain, that they may live.'" ¹⁰ So I prophesied as he commanded me, and breath entered them; they came to life and stood up on their feet—a vast army. ¹¹ Then he said to me: "Son of man, these bones are the whole house of Israel. They say, 'Our bones are dried up and our hope is gone: we are cut off.' ¹² "Therefore prophesy and say to them: 'This is what the Sovereign Lord says: O my people, I am going to open your grave and bring you up to them; I

will bring you back to the land of Israel. [13] "'Then you, my people, will know that I am the Lord, when I open your graves and bring you up from them. [14] "'I will put my Spirit in you and you will live, and I will settle you in your own land. Then you will know that I the Lord have spoken, and I have done it, declares the Lord.'"

ONE NATION UNDER ONE KING

[15] The word of the Lord came to me: [16] "Son of man, take a stick of wood, and write on it, 'Belonging to Judah and the Israelites associated with him.' Then take another stick of wood and write on it, 'Ephraim's stick, belong to Joseph and all the house of Israel associated with him.' [17] "Join them together into one stick so that they will become one in your hand. [18] "When your countrymen ask you, 'Won't you tell us what you mean by this?' [19] "Say to them, 'This is what the Sovereign Lord says: I am going to take the stick of Joseph—which is in Ephraim's hand—and of the Israelite tribes associated with him, and join it to Judah's stick, making them a single stick of wood, and they will become one in my hand.' [20] "Hold before their eyes the stick you have written on. [21] "And say to them, 'This is what the Sovereign Lord says: I will take the Israelites out of the nations where they have gone. I will gather them from all around and bring them back into their own land. [22] "'I will make them one nation in the land, on the mountains of Israel. There will be one king over all of them and they will never again be two nations or be divided into two kingdoms. [23] "'They will no longer defile themselves with their idols and vile images or with any of their offences, for I will save them from all their sinful backsliding and I will cleanse them. They will be my people, and I will be their God. [24] "'My servant David will be king over them, and they will all have one shepherd. They will follow my laws and be careful to

keep my decrees. ²⁵ "'They will live in the land I gave to my servant Jacob, the land where your fathers lived. They and their children and their children's children will live there forever, and David my servant will be their prince for ever. ²⁶ "'I will make a covenant of peace with them; it will be an everlasting covenant. I will establish them and increase their numbers, and I will put my sanctuary among them forever. ²⁷ "'My dwelling-place will be with them; I will be their God, and they will be my people. Then the nations will know that I the Lord make Israel holy, when my sanctuary is among them forever.'"

Chapter 38

A PROPHECY AGAINST GOG

¹ The word of the Lord came to me: ² "Son of man, set your face against Gog, of the land of Magog, the chief prince of Meshech and Tubal; prophesy against him ³ "and say: 'This is what the Sovereign Lord says: I am against you, O Gog, chief prince of Meshech and Tubal. ⁴ "'I will turn you around, put hooks in your jaws and bring you out with your whole army—your horses, your horsemen fully armed, and a great horde with large and small shields, all of them brandishing their swords. ⁵ "'Persia, Cush and Put will be with them, all with shields and helmets, ⁶ "'also Gomer with all its troops, and Beth Togarmah from the far north with all its troops— the many nations with you. ⁷ "'Get ready; be prepared, you and all the hordes gathered about you, and take command of them. ⁸ "'After many days you will be called to arms. In future years you will invade a land that has recovered from war, whose people were gathered from many nations to the mountains of Israel, which had long been desolate. They had been brought out from the nations, and now all of them live in safety. ⁹ "'You and all your troops, and

the many nations with you will go up, advancing like a storm; you will be like a cloud covering the land. ¹⁰ "'This is what the Sovereign Lords says: On that day thoughts will come into your mind and you will devise an evil scheme. ¹¹ "'You will say, "I will invade a land of unwalled villages: I will attack a peaceful and unsuspecting people—all of them living without walls and without gates and bars. ¹² "'I will plunder and loot and turn my hand against the resettled ruins and the people gathered from the nations, rich in livestock and goods, living at the centre of the land.'" ¹³ "'Sheba and Dedan and the merchants of Tarshish and all her villages will say to you, "Have you come to plunder? Have you gathered you hordes to loot, to carry off silver and gold, to take away livestock and goods and to seize much plunder?"' ¹⁴ "Therefore, son of man, prophesy and say to Gog: 'This is what the Sovereign Lord says: In that day, when my people Israel are living in safety, will you not take notice of it? ¹⁵ "'You will come from your place in the far north, you and many nations with you, all of them riding on horses, a great horde, a mighty army. ¹⁶ "'You will advance against my people Israel like a cloud that covers the land. In days to come, O Gog, I will bring you against my land, so that the nations may know me when I show myself holy through you before their eyes." ¹⁷ "'This is what the Sovereign Lord says: Are you not the one I spoke of in former days by my servants the prophets of Israel? At that time they prophesied for years that I would bring you against them. ¹⁸ "'This is what will happen in that day: When Gog attacks the land of Israel, my hot anger will be aroused, declares the Sovereign Lord. ¹⁹ "'In my zeal and fiery wrath I declare that at that time there shall be a great earthquake in the land of Israel. ²⁰ "'The fish of the sea, the birds of the air, the beasts of the field, every creature that moves along the ground, and all the people on the face of the earth will tremble at my presence. The mountains will be overturned, the cliffs will crumble and every wall will fall to the ground. [21] "'I will summon a sword against Gog on all my mountains, declares the Sovereign Lord. Every man's sword will be against his brother. [22] "'I will execute judgement upon him with plague and bloodshed; I will pour down torrents of rain, hailstones and burning sulphur on him and on his troops and on the many nations with him. [23] "'And so I will show my greatness and my holiness, and I will make myself known in the sight of many nations. Then they will know that I am the Lord.'

Chapter 39

[1] "Son of man, prophesy against Gog and say: 'This is what the Sovereign Lord says: I am against you, O Gog, chief prince of Meshech and Tubal. [2] "'I will turn you around and drag you along. I will bring you from the far north and send you against the mountains of Israel. [3] "'Then I will strike your bow from your left hand and make your arrows drop from your right hand. 4 "'On the mountains of Israel you will fall, you and all your troops and the nations with you. I will give you as food to all kinds of carrion birds and to the wild animals. [5] "'You will fall in the open field, for I have spoken, declares the Sovereign Lord. [6] "'I will send fire on Magog and on those who live in safety in the coastlands, and they will know that I am the Lord. [7] "'I will make known my holy name among my people Israel. I will no longer let my holy name be profaned and the nations will know that I the Lord am the Holy One in Israel. [8] "'It is coming! It will surely take place, declares the Sovereign Lord. This is the day I have spoken of. [9] "'Then those who live in the towns of Israel will go out and use the weapons for fuel and burn

them up—the small and large shields, the bows and arrows, the war clubs and spears. For seven years they will use them for fuel. [10] "'They will not need to gather wood from the fields or cut it from the forest, because they will use the weapons for fuel. And they will plunder those who plundered them and loot those who looted them, declares the Sovereign Lord. [11] "'On that day I will give Gog a burial place in Israel, in the valley of those who travel east toward the Sea. It will block the way of travelers, because Gog and all his hordes will be buried there. So it will be called the Valley of Hamon Gog. [12] "'For seven months the house of Israel will be burying them in order to cleanse the land. [13] "'All the people of the land will bury them, and the day I am glorified will be a memorable day for them, declares the Sovereign Lord. [14] "'Men will be regularly employed to cleanse the land. Some will go throughout the land and, in addition to them, others will bury those that remain on the ground. At the end of the seven months they will begin their search. [15] "'As they go through the land and one of them sees a human bone, he will set up a marker beside it until the gravediggers have buried it in the Valley of Hamon Gog. [16] "'(Also a town called Hamonah will be there.) And so they will cleanse the land.' [17] "Son of man, this is what the Sovereign Lord says: Call out to every kind of bird and all the wild animals: 'Assemble and come together from all around to the sacrifice I am preparing for you, the great sacrifice on the mountains of Israel. There you will eat flesh and drink blood. [18] "You will eat the flesh of mighty men and drink the blood of the princes of the earth as if they were rams and lambs, goats and bulls—all of them fattened animals from Bashan. [19] "At the sacrifice I am preparing for you, you will eat fat till you are glutted and drink blood till you are drunk. [20] "At my table you will eat your fill of horses and riders, mighty men and soldiers of every kind,' declares the Sovereign Lord. [21] "I will display my glory among the nations, and all the nations will see the punishment I inflict and the hand I lay upon them. [22] "From that day forward the house of Israel will know that I am the Lord their God. [23] "And the nations will know that the people of Israel went into exile for their sin, because they were unfaithful to me. So I hid my face from them and handed them over to their enemies, and they all fell by the sword. [24] "I dealt with them according to their uncleanness and their offences, and I hid my face from them. [25] "Therefore this is what the Sovereign Lord says: I will now bring Jacob back from captivity and will have compassion on all the people of Israel, and I will be zealous for my holy name. [26] "They will forget their shame and all the unfaithfulness they showed toward me when they lived in safety in their land with no one to make them afraid. [27] "When I have brought them back from the nations and have gathered them from the countries of their enemies, I will show myself holy through them in the sight of many nations. [28] "Then they will know that I am the Lord their God, for though I sent them into exile among the nations, I will gather them to their own land, not leaving any behind. [29] "I will no longer hide my face from them, for I will pour out my spirit on the house of Israel, declares the Sovereign Lord."

Book of Daniel
Written 495 BC

Chapter 7

[1] In the first year of Belshazzar king of Babylon, Daniel had a dream, and visions passed through his mind as he was lying on his bed. He wrote down the substance of his dream. [2] Daniel said: "In my vision at night I looked, and there before me were the four winds of heaven churning up the great sea. [3] "Four great beasts, each different from the others, came up out of the sea. [4] "The first was like a lion, and it had the wings of an eagle. I watched until its wings were torn off and it was lifted from the ground so that it stood on two feet like a man, and the heart of a man was given to it. [5] "And there before me was a second beast, which looked like a bear. It was raised up on one of its sides, and it had three ribs in its mouth between its teeth. It was told, 'Get up and eat your fill of flesh!' [6] "After that, I looked, and there before me was another beast, one that looked like a leopard. And on its back it had four wings like those of a bird. This beast had four heads, and it was given authority to rule. [7] "After that, in my vision at night I looked, and there before me was a fourth beast—terrifying and frightening and very powerful. It had large iron teeth; it crushed and devoured its victims and trampled underfoot whatever was left. It was different from all the former beasts, and it had ten horns. [8] "While I was thinking about the horns, there before me was another horn, a little one, which came up among them; and three of the first horns were uprooted before it. This horn had eyes like the eyes of a man and a mouth that spoke boastfully. [9] "As I looked, / thrones were set in place,/ and the Ancient of Days / took his seat. / His clothing was as white as snow; / the hair of his head was white like wool. / His throne was

flaming with fire, / and its wheels were all ablaze. // [10] "A river of fire was flowing, / coming out from before him. / Thousands upon thousands attended him; / ten thousand times ten thousand stood before him. / The court was seated, / and the books were opened. [11] "Then I continued to watch because of the boastful words the horn was speaking. I kept looking until the beast was slain and its body destroyed and thrown into the blazing fire. [12] "(The other beasts had been stripped of their authority, but were allowed to live for a period of time.) [13] "In my vision at night I looked, and there before me was one like a son of man, coming with the clouds of heaven. He approached the Ancient of Days and was led into his presence. [14] "He was given authority, glory and sovereign power; all peoples, nations and men of every language worshiped him. His dominion is an everlasting dominion that will not pass away, and his kingdom is one that will never be destroyed.

The Interpretation Of The Dream

[15] "I, Daniel, was troubled in spirit, and the visions that passed through my mind disturbed me. [16] "I approached one of those standing there and asked him the true meaning of all this. So he told me and gave me the interpretation of these things. [17] "'The four great beasts are four kingdoms that will rise from the earth. [18] "'But the saints of the Most High will receive the kingdom and will possess it forever—yes, forever and ever.' [19] "Then I wanted to know the true meaning of the fourth beast, which was different from all the others and most terrifying, with its iron teeth and bronze claws—the beast that crushed and devoured its victims and trampled underfoot whatever was left. [20] "I also wanted to know about the ten horns on its head and about the other horn that came up, before which three of them fell—the horn that looked more

imposing than the others and that had eyes and a mouth that spoke boastfully. [21] "As I watched, this horn was waging war against the saints and defeating them. [22] "Until the Ancient of Days came and pronounced judgement in favour of the saints of the Most High, and the time came when they possessed the kingdom. [23] "He gave me this explanation: 'The fourth beast is a fourth kingdom that will appear on earth. It will be different from all the other kingdoms and will devour the whole earth, trampling it down and crushing it. [24] "'The ten horns are ten kings who will come from this kingdom. After them another king will arise, different from the earlier ones; he will subdue three kings. [25] "'He will speak against the Most High and oppress his saints and try to change the set times and the laws. The saints will be handed over to him for a time, times and half a time. [26] "'But the court will sit, and his power will be taken away and completely destroyed for ever. [27] "'Then the sovereignty, power and greatness of the kingdoms under the whole heaven will be handed over to the saints, the people of the Most High. His kingdom will be an everlasting kingdom, and all rulers will worship and obey him.' [28] "This is the end of the matter. I, Daniel, was deeply troubled by my thoughts, and my face turned pale, but I kept the matter to myself."

Book of Revelation
King James Version
(Note: This is the only excerpt taken from the King James Version. All other excerpts in Appendix C and all quotations cited throughout the book are taken from the New International Version.)
Written circa AD 96

Revelation 1

1 The Revelation of Jesus Christ, which God gave unto him, to shew unto his servants things which must shortly come to pass; and he sent and signified it by his angel unto his servant John: 2 Who bare record of the word of God, and of the testimony of Jesus Christ, and of all things that he saw. 3 Blessed is he that readeth, and they that hear the words of this prophecy, and keep those things which are written therein: for the time is at hand. 4 John to the seven churches which are in Asia: Grace be unto you, and peace, from him which is, and which was, and which is to come; and from the seven Spirits which are before his throne; 5 And from Jesus Christ, who is the faithful witness, and the first begotten of the dead, and the prince of the kings of the earth. Unto him that loved us, and washed us from our sins in his own blood, 6 And hath made us kings and priests unto God and his Father; to him be glory and dominion for ever and ever. Amen. 7 Behold, he cometh with clouds; and every eye shall see him, and they also which pierced him: and all kindreds of the earth shall wail because of him. Even so, Amen. 8 I am Alpha and Omega, the beginning and the ending, saith the Lord, which is, and which was, and which is to come, the Almighty. 9 I John, who also am your brother, and companion in tribulation, and in the kingdom and patience of Jesus Christ, was in the isle that is called Patmos, for the word of God, and for the

testimony of Jesus Christ. [10] I was in the Spirit on the Lord's day, and heard behind me a great voice, as of a trumpet, [11] Saying, I am Alpha and Omega, the first and the last: and, What thou seest, write in a book, and send it unto the seven churches which are in Asia; unto Ephesus, and unto Smyrna, and unto Pergamos, and unto Thyatira, and unto Sardis, and unto Philadelphia, and unto Laodicea. [12] And I turned to see the voice that spake with me. And being turned, I saw seven golden candlesticks; [13] And in the midst of the seven candlesticks one like unto the Son of man, clothed with a garment down to the foot, and girt about the paps with a golden girdle. [14] His head and his hairs were white like wool, as white as snow; and his eyes were as a flame of fire; [15] And his feet like unto fine brass, as if they burned in a furnace; and his voice as the sound of many waters. [16] And he had in his right hand seven stars: and out of his mouth went a sharp twoedged sword: and his countenance was as the sun shineth in his strength. [17] And when I saw him, I fell at his feet as dead. And he laid his right hand upon me, saying unto me, Fear not; I am the first and the last: [18] I am he that liveth, and was dead; and, behold, I am alive for evermore, Amen; and have the keys of hell and of death. [19] Write the things which thou hast seen, and the things which are, and the things which shall be hereafter; [20] The mystery of the seven stars which thou sawest in my right hand, and the seven golden candlesticks. The seven stars are the angels of the seven churches: and the seven candlesticks which thou sawest are the seven churches.

Revelation 2

[1] Unto the angel of the church of Ephesus write; These things saith he that holdeth the seven stars in his right hand, who walketh in the midst of the seven golden candlesticks; [2] I know thy works,

and thy labour, and thy patience, and how thou canst not bear them which are evil: and thou hast tried them which say they are apostles, and are not, and hast found them liars: [3] And hast borne, and hast patience, and for my name's sake hast laboured, and hast not fainted. [4] Nevertheless I have somewhat against thee, because thou hast left thy first love. [5] Remember therefore from whence thou art fallen, and repent, and do the first works; or else I will come unto thee quickly, and will remove thy candlestick out of his place, except thou repent. [6] But this thou hast, that thou hatest the deeds of the Nicolaitanes, which I also hate. [7] He that hath an ear, let him hear what the Spirit saith unto the churches; To him that overcometh will I give to eat of the tree of life, which is in the midst of the paradise of God. [8] And unto the angel of the church in Smyrna write; These things saith the first and the last, which was dead, and is alive; [9] I know thy works, and tribulation, and poverty, (but thou art rich) and I know the blasphemy of them which say they are Jews, and are not, but are the synagogue of Satan. [10] Fear none of those things which thou shalt suffer: behold, the devil shall cast some of you into prison, that ye may be tried; and ye shall have tribulation ten days: be thou faithful unto death, and I will give thee a crown of life. [11] He that hath an ear, let him hear what the Spirit saith unto the churches; He that overcometh shall not be hurt of the second death. [12] And to the angel of the church in Pergamos write; These things saith he which hath the sharp sword with two edges; [13] I know thy works, and where thou dwellest, even where Satan's seat is: and thou holdest fast my name, and hast not denied my faith, even in those days wherein Antipas was my faithful martyr, who was slain among you, where Satan dwelleth. [14] But I have a few things against thee, because thou hast there them that hold the doctrine of Balaam, who taught Balac to cast a stumblingblock before the children of Israel, to eat things sacrificed unto idols, and to commit fornication. [15] So hast thou also them that hold the doctrine of the Nicolaitanes, which thing I hate. [16] Repent; or else I will come unto thee quickly, and will fight against them with the sword of my mouth. [17] He that hath an ear, let him hear what the Spirit saith unto the churches; To him that overcometh will I give to eat of the hidden manna, and will give him a white stone, and in the stone a new name written, which no man knoweth saving he that receiveth it. [18] And unto the angel of the church in Thyatira write; These things saith the Son of God, who hath his eyes like unto a flame of fire, and his feet are like fine brass; [19] I know thy works, and charity, and service, and faith, and thy patience, and thy works; and the last to be more than the first. [20] Notwithstanding I have a few things against thee, because thou sufferest that woman Jezebel, which calleth herself a prophetess, to teach and to seduce my servants to commit fornication, and to eat things sacrificed unto idols. [21] And I gave her space to repent of her fornication; and she repented not. [22] Behold, I will cast her into a bed, and them that commit adultery with her into great tribulation, except they repent of their deeds. 23 And I will kill her children with death; and all the churches shall know that I am he which searcheth the reins and hearts: and I will give unto every one of you according to your works. [24] But unto you I say, and unto the rest in Thyatira, as many as have not this doctrine, and which have not known the depths of Satan, as they speak; I will put upon you none other burden. [25] But that which ye have already hold fast till I come. [26] And he that overcometh, and keepeth my works unto the end, to him will I give power over the nations: [27] And he shall rule them with a rod of iron; as the vessels of a potter shall they be broken to shivers: even as I received of my Father. [28] And I will give him the morning star. [29] He that hath an ear, let him hear what the Spirit saith unto the churches.

Revelation 3

[1] And unto the angel of the church in Sardis write; These things saith he that hath the seven Spirits of God, and the seven stars; I know thy works, that thou hast a name that thou livest, and art dead. [2] Be watchful, and strengthen the things which remain, that are ready to die: for I have not found thy works perfect before God. [3] Remember therefore how thou hast received and heard, and hold fast, and repent. If therefore thou shalt not watch, I will come on thee as a thief, and thou shalt not know what hour I will come upon thee. [4] Thou hast a few names even in Sardis which have not defiled their garments; and they shall walk with me in white: for they are worthy. [5] He that overcometh, the same shall be clothed in white raiment; and I will not blot out his name out of the book of life, but I will confess his name before my Father, and before his angels. [6] He that hath an ear, let him hear what the Spirit saith unto the churches. [7] And to the angel of the church in Philadelphia write; These things saith he that is holy, he that is true, he that hath the key of David, he that openeth, and no man shutteth; and shutteth, and no man openeth; [8] I know thy works: behold, I have set before thee an open door, and no man can shut it: for thou hast a little strength, and hast kept my word, and hast not denied my name. [9] Behold, I will make them of the synagogue of Satan, which say they are Jews, and are not, but do lie; behold, I will make them to come and worship before thy feet, and to know that I have loved thee. [10] Because thou hast kept the word of my patience, I also will

keep thee from the hour of temptation, which shall come upon all the world, to try them that dwell upon the earth. [11] Behold, I come quickly: hold that fast which thou hast, that no man take thy crown. [12] Him that overcometh will I make a pillar in the temple of my God, and he shall go no more out: and I will write upon him the name of my God, and the name of the city of my God, which is new Jerusalem, which cometh down out of heaven from my God: and I will write upon him my new name. [13] He that hath an ear, let him hear what the Spirit saith unto the churches. [14] And unto the angel of the church of the Laodiceans write; These things saith the Amen, the faithful and true witness, the beginning of the creation of God; [15] I know thy works, that thou art neither cold nor hot: I would thou wert cold or hot. [16] So then because thou art lukewarm, and neither cold nor hot, I will spue thee out of my mouth. [17] Because thou sayest, I am rich, and increased with goods, and have need of nothing; and knowest not that thou art wretched, and miserable, and poor, and blind, and naked: [18] I counsel thee to buy of me gold tried in the fire, that thou mayest be rich; and white raiment, that thou mayest be clothed, and that the shame of thy nakedness do not appear; and anoint thine eyes with eyesalve, that thou mayest see. [19] As many as I love, I rebuke and chasten: be zealous therefore, and repent. [20] Behold, I stand at the door, and knock: if any man hear my voice, and open the door, I will come in to him, and will sup with him, and he with me. [21] To him that overcometh will I grant to sit with me in my throne, even as I also overcame, and am set down with my Father in his throne. [22] He that hath an ear, let him hear what the Spirit saith unto the churches.

Revelation 4

[1] After this I looked, and, behold, a door was opened in heaven: and the first voice which I heard was as it were of a trumpet talking with me; which said, Come up hither, and I will shew thee things which must be hereafter. [2] And immediately I was in the spirit: and, behold, a throne was set in heaven, and one sat on the throne. [3] And he that sat was to look upon like a jasper and a sardine stone: and there was a rainbow round about the throne, in sight like unto an emerald. [4] And round about the throne were four and twenty seats: and upon the seats I saw four and twenty elders sitting, clothed in white raiment; and they had on their heads crowns of gold. [5] And out of the throne proceeded lightnings and thunderings and voices: and there were seven lamps of fire burning before the throne, which are the seven Spirits of God. [6] And before the throne there was a sea of glass like unto crystal: and in the midst of the throne, and round about the throne, were four beasts full of eyes before and behind. [7] And the first beast was like a lion, and the second beast like a calf, and the third beast had a face as a man, and the fourth beast was like a flying eagle. [8] And the four beasts had each of them six wings about him; and they were full of eyes within: and they rest not day and night, saying, Holy, holy, holy, LORD God Almighty, which was, and is, and is to come. [9] And when those beasts give glory and honour and thanks to him that sat on the throne, who liveth for ever and ever, [10] The four and twenty elders fall down before him that sat on the throne, and worship him that liveth for ever and ever, and cast their crowns before the throne, saying, [11] Thou art worthy, O Lord, to receive glory and honour and power: for thou hast created all things, and for thy pleasure they are and were created.

Revelation 5

[1] And I saw in the right hand of him that sat on the throne a book written within and on the backside, sealed with seven seals. [2] And I saw a strong angel proclaiming with a loud voice, Who is worthy to open the book, and to loose the seals thereof? [3] And no man in heaven, nor in earth, neither under the earth, was able to open the book, neither to look thereon. [4] And I wept much, because no man was found worthy to open and to read the book, neither to look thereon. [5] And one of the elders saith unto me, Weep not: behold, the Lion of the tribe of Judah, the Root of David, hath prevailed to open the book, and to loose the seven seals thereof. [6] And I beheld, and, lo, in the midst of the throne and of the four beasts, and in the midst of the elders, stood a Lamb as it had been slain, having seven horns and seven eyes, which are the seven Spirits of God sent forth into all the earth. [7] And he came and took the book out of the right hand of him that sat upon the throne. [8] And when he had taken the book, the four beasts and four and twenty elders fell down before the Lamb, having every one of them harps, and golden vials full of odours, which are the prayers of saints. [9] And they sung a new song, saying, Thou art worthy to take the book, and to open the seals thereof: for thou wast slain, and hast redeemed us to God by thy blood out of every kindred, and tongue, and people, and nation; [10] And hast made us unto our God kings and priests: and we shall reign on the earth. [11] And I beheld, and I heard the voice of many angels round about the throne and the beasts and the elders: and the number of them was ten thousand times ten thousand, and thousands of thousands; [12] Saying with a loud voice, Worthy is the Lamb that was slain to receive power, and riches, and wisdom, and strength, and honour, and glory, and blessing. [13] And every creature

which is in heaven, and on the earth, and under the earth, and such as are in the sea, and all that are in them, heard I saying, Blessing, and honour, and glory, and power, be unto him that sitteth upon the throne, and unto the Lamb for ever and ever. [14] And the four beasts said, Amen. And the four and twenty elders fell down and worshipped him that liveth for ever and ever.

Revelation 6

[1] And I saw when the Lamb opened one of the seals, and I heard, as it were the noise of thunder, one of the four beasts saying, Come and see. [2] And I saw, and behold a white horse: and he that sat on him had a bow; and a crown was given unto him: and he went forth conquering, and to conquer. [3] And when he had opened the second seal, I heard the second beast say, Come and see. [4] And there went out another horse that was red: and power was given to him that sat thereon to take peace from the earth, and that they should kill one another: and there was given unto him a great sword. [5] And when he had opened the third seal, I heard the third beast say, Come and see. And I beheld, and lo a black horse; and he that sat on him had a pair of balances in his hand. [6] And I heard a voice in the midst of the four beasts say, A measure of wheat for a penny, and three measures of barley for a penny; and see thou hurt not the oil and the wine. [7] And when he had opened the fourth seal, I heard the voice of the fourth beast say, Come and see. [8] And I looked, and behold a pale horse: and his name that sat on him was Death, and Hell followed with him. And power was given unto them over the fourth part of the earth, to kill with sword, and with hunger, and with death, and with the beasts of the earth. [9] And when he had opened the fifth seal, I saw under the altar the souls of them that were slain for the word of God, and for the testimony which they

held: [10] And they cried with a loud voice, saying, How long, O Lord, holy and true, dost thou not judge and avenge our blood on them that dwell on the earth? [11] And white robes were given unto every one of them; and it was said unto them, that they should rest yet for a little season, until their fellowservants also and their brethren, that should be killed as they were, should be fulfilled. [12] And I beheld when he had opened the sixth seal, and, lo, there was a great earthquake; and the sun became black as sackcloth of hair, and the moon became as blood; [13] And the stars of heaven fell unto the earth, even as a fig tree casteth her untimely figs, when she is shaken of a mighty wind. [14] And the heaven departed as a scroll when it is rolled together; and every mountain and island were moved out of their places. [15] And the kings of the earth, and the great men, and the rich men, and the chief captains, and the mighty men, and every bondman, and every free man, hid themselves in the dens and in the rocks of the mountains; [16] And said to the mountains and rocks, Fall on us, and hide us from the face of him that sitteth on the throne, and from the wrath of the Lamb: [17] For the great day of his wrath is come; and who shall be able to stand?

Revelation 7

[1] And after these things I saw four angels standing on the four corners of the earth, holding the four winds of the earth, that the wind should not blow on the earth, nor on the sea, nor on any tree. [2] And I saw another angel ascending from the east, having the seal of the living God: and he cried with a loud voice to the four angels, to whom it was given to hurt the earth and the sea, [3] Saying, Hurt not the earth, neither the sea, nor the trees, till we have sealed the servants of our God in their foreheads. [4] And I heard the number of them which were sealed: and there were sealed an hundred and

forty and four thousand of all the tribes of the children of Israel. [5] Of the tribe of Juda were sealed twelve thousand. Of the tribe of Reuben were sealed twelve thousand. Of the tribe of Gad were sealed twelve thousand. [6] Of the tribe of Aser were sealed twelve thousand. Of the tribe of Nephthalim were sealed twelve thousand. Of the tribe of Manasses were sealed twelve thousand. [7] Of the tribe of Simeon were sealed twelve thousand. Of the tribe of Levi were sealed twelve thousand. Of the tribe of Issachar were sealed twelve thousand. [8] Of the tribe of Zabulon were sealed twelve thousand. Of the tribe of Joseph were sealed twelve thousand. Of the tribe of Benjamin were sealed twelve thousand. [9] After this I beheld, and, lo, a great multitude, which no man could number, of all nations, and kindreds, and people, and tongues, stood before the throne, and before the Lamb, clothed with white robes, and palms in their hands; [10] And cried with a loud voice, saying, Salvation to our God which sitteth upon the throne, and unto the Lamb. [11] And all the angels stood round about the throne, and about the elders and the four beasts, and fell before the throne on their faces, and worshipped God, [12] Saying, Amen: Blessing, and glory, and wisdom, and thanksgiving, and honour, and power, and might, be unto our God for ever and ever. Amen. [13] And one of the elders answered, saying unto me, What are these which are arrayed in white robes? and whence came they? [14] And I said unto him, Sir, thou knowest. And he said to me, These are they which came out of great tribulation, and have washed their robes, and made them white in the blood of the Lamb. [15] Therefore are they before the throne of God, and serve him day and night in his temple: and he that sitteth on the throne shall dwell among them. [16] They shall hunger no more, neither thirst any more; neither shall the sun light on them, nor any heat. [17] For the Lamb which is in the midst of the throne shall feed them, and shall lead them unto living fountains of waters: and God shall wipe away all tears from their eyes.

Revelation 8

[1] And when he had opened the seventh seal, there was silence in heaven about the space of half an hour. [2] And I saw the seven angels which stood before God; and to them were given seven trumpets. [3] And another angel came and stood at the altar, having a golden censer; and there was given unto him much incense, that he should offer it with the prayers of all saints upon the golden altar which was before the throne. [4] And the smoke of the incense, which came with the prayers of the saints, ascended up before God out of the angel's hand. [5] And the angel took the censer, and filled it with fire of the altar, and cast it into the earth: and there were voices, and thunderings, and lightnings, and an earthquake. [6] And the seven angels which had the seven trumpets prepared themselves to sound. [7] The first angel sounded, and there followed hail and fire mingled with blood, and they were cast upon the earth: and the third part of trees was burnt up, and all green grass was burnt up. [8] And the second angel sounded, and as it were a great mountain burning with fire was cast into the sea: and the third part of the sea became blood; [9] And the third part of the creatures which were in the sea, and had life, died; and the third part of the ships were destroyed. [10] And the third angel sounded, and there fell a great star from heaven, burning as it were a lamp, and it fell upon the third part of the rivers, and upon the fountains of waters; [11] And the name of the star is called Wormwood: and the third part of the waters became wormwood; and many men died of the waters, because they were made bitter. [12] And the fourth angel sounded, and the third part of

the sun was smitten, and the third part of the moon, and the third part of the stars; so as the third part of them was darkened, and the day shone not for a third part of it, and the night likewise. [13] And I beheld, and heard an angel flying through the midst of heaven, saying with a loud voice, Woe, woe, woe, to the inhabiters of the earth by reason of the other voices of the trumpet of the three angels, which are yet to sound!

Revelation 9

[1] And the fifth angel sounded, and I saw a star fall from heaven unto the earth: and to him was given the key of the bottomless pit. [2] And he opened the bottomless pit; and there arose a smoke out of the pit, as the smoke of a great furnace; and the sun and the air were darkened by reason of the smoke of the pit. [3] And there came out of the smoke locusts upon the earth: and unto them was given power, as the scorpions of the earth have power. [4] And it was commanded them that they should not hurt the grass of the earth, neither any green thing, neither any tree; but only those men which have not the seal of God in their foreheads. [5] And to them it was given that they should not kill them, but that they should be tormented five months: and their torment was as the torment of a scorpion, when he striketh a man. [6] And in those days shall men seek death, and shall not find it; and shall desire to die, and death shall flee from them. [7] And the shapes of the locusts were like unto horses prepared unto battle; and on their heads were as it were crowns like gold, and their faces were as the faces of men. [8] And they had hair as the hair of women, and their teeth were as the teeth of lions. [9] And they had breastplates, as it were breastplates of iron; and the sound of their wings was as the sound of chariots of many horses running to battle. [10] And they had tails like unto scor-

pions, and there were stings in their tails: and their power was to hurt men five months. [11] And they had a king over them, which is the angel of the bottomless pit, whose name in the Hebrew tongue is Abaddon, but in the Greek tongue hath his name Apollyon. [12] One woe is past; and, behold, there come two woes more hereafter. [13] And the sixth angel sounded, and I heard a voice from the four horns of the golden altar which is before God, [14] Saying to the sixth angel which had the trumpet, Loose the four angels which are bound in the great river Euphrates. [15] And the four angels were loosed, which were prepared for an hour, and a day, and a month, and a year, for to slay the third part of men. [16] And the number of the army of the horsemen were two hundred thousand thousand: and I heard the number of them. [17] And thus I saw the horses in the vision, and them that sat on them, having breastplates of fire, and of jacinth, and brimstone: and the heads of the horses were as the heads of lions; and out of their mouths issued fire and smoke and brimstone. [18] By these three was the third part of men killed, by the fire, and by the smoke, and by the brimstone, which issued out of their mouths. [19] For their power is in their mouth, and in their tails: for their tails were like unto serpents, and had heads, and with them they do hurt. [20] And the rest of the men which were not killed by these plagues yet repented not of the works of their hands, that they should not worship devils, and idols of gold, and silver, and brass, and stone, and of wood: which neither can see, nor hear, nor walk: [21] Neither repented they of their murders, nor of their sorceries, nor of their fornication, nor of their thefts.

Revelation 10

[1] And I saw another mighty angel come down from heaven, clothed with a cloud: and a rainbow was upon his head, and his face was

as it were the sun, and his feet as pillars of fire: [2] And he had in his hand a little book open: and he set his right foot upon the sea, and his left foot on the earth, [3] And cried with a loud voice, as when a lion roareth: and when he had cried, seven thunders uttered their voices. [4] And when the seven thunders had uttered their voices, I was about to write: and I heard a voice from heaven saying unto me, Seal up those things which the seven thunders uttered, and write them not. [5] And the angel which I saw stand upon the sea and upon the earth lifted up his hand to heaven, [6] And sware by him that liveth for ever and ever, who created heaven, and the things that therein are, and the earth, and the things that therein are, and the sea, and the things which are therein, that there should be time no longer: [7] But in the days of the voice of the seventh angel, when he shall begin to sound, the mystery of God should be finished, as he hath declared to his servants the prophets. [8] And the voice which I heard from heaven spake unto me again, and said, Go and take the little book which is open in the hand of the angel which standeth upon the sea and upon the earth. [9] And I went unto the angel, and said unto him, Give me the little book. And he said unto me, Take it, and eat it up; and it shall make thy belly bitter, but it shall be in thy mouth sweet as honey. [10] And I took the little book out of the angel's hand, and ate it up; and it was in my mouth sweet as honey: and as soon as I had eaten it, my belly was bitter. [11] And he said unto me, Thou must prophesy again before many peoples, and nations, and tongues, and kings.

Revelation 11

[1] And there was given me a reed like unto a rod: and the angel stood, saying, Rise, and measure the temple of God, and the altar, and them that worship therein. [2] But the court which is without

the temple leave out, and measure it not; for it is given unto the Gentiles: and the holy city shall they tread under foot forty and two months. ³ And I will give power unto my two witnesses, and they shall prophesy a thousand two hundred and threescore days, clothed in sackcloth. ⁴ These are the two olive trees, and the two candlesticks standing before the God of the earth. ⁵ And if any man will hurt them, fire proceedeth out of their mouth, and devoureth their enemies: and if any man will hurt them, he must in this manner be killed. ⁶ These have power to shut heaven, that it rain not in the days of their prophecy: and have power over waters to turn them to blood, and to smite the earth with all plagues, as often as they will. ⁷ And when they shall have finished their testimony, the beast that ascendeth out of the bottomless pit shall make war against them, and shall overcome them, and kill them. ⁸ And their dead bodies shall lie in the street of the great city, which spiritually is called Sodom and Egypt, where also our Lord was crucified. ⁹ And they of the people and kindreds and tongues and nations shall see their dead bodies three days and an half, and shall not suffer their dead bodies to be put in graves. ¹⁰ And they that dwell upon the earth shall rejoice over them, and make merry, and shall send gifts one to another; because these two prophets tormented them that dwelt on the earth. ¹¹ And after three days and an half the spirit of life from God entered into them, and they stood upon their feet; and great fear fell upon them which saw them. ¹² And they heard a great voice from heaven saying unto them, Come up hither. And they ascended up to heaven in a cloud; and their enemies beheld them. ¹³ And the same hour was there a great earthquake, and the tenth part of the city fell, and in the earthquake were slain of men seven thousand: and the remnant were affrighted, and gave glory to the God of heaven. [14] The second woe is past; and, behold, the third woe cometh quickly. [15] And the seventh angel sounded; and there were great voices in heaven, saying, The kingdoms of this world are become the kingdoms of our Lord, and of his Christ; and he shall reign for ever and ever. [16] And the four and twenty elders, which sat before God on their seats, fell upon their faces, and worshipped God, [17] Saying, We give thee thanks, O LORD God Almighty, which art, and wast, and art to come; because thou hast taken to thee thy great power, and hast reigned. [18] And the nations were angry, and thy wrath is come, and the time of the dead, that they should be judged, and that thou shouldest give reward unto thy servants the prophets, and to the saints, and them that fear thy name, small and great; and shouldest destroy them which destroy the earth. [19] And the temple of God was opened in heaven, and there was seen in his temple the ark of his testament: and there were lightnings, and voices, and thunderings, and an earthquake, and great hail.

Revelation 12

[1] And there appeared a great wonder in heaven; a woman clothed with the sun, and the moon under her feet, and upon her head a crown of twelve stars: [2] And she being with child cried, travailing in birth, and pained to be delivered. [3] And there appeared another wonder in heaven; and behold a great red dragon, having seven heads and ten horns, and seven crowns upon his heads. [4] And his tail drew the third part of the stars of heaven, and did cast them to the earth: and the dragon stood before the woman which was ready to be delivered, for to devour her child as soon as it was born. [5] And she brought forth a man child, who was to rule all nations with a rod of iron: and her child was caught up unto God, and to his

throne. ⁶ And the woman fled into the wilderness, where she hath a place prepared of God, that they should feed her there a thousand two hundred and threescore days. ⁷ And there was war in heaven: Michael and his angels fought against the dragon; and the dragon fought and his angels, ⁸ And prevailed not; neither was their place found any more in heaven. ⁹ And the great dragon was cast out, that old serpent, called the Devil, and Satan, which deceiveth the whole world: he was cast out into the earth, and his angels were cast out with him. ¹⁰ And I heard a loud voice saying in heaven, Now is come salvation, and strength, and the kingdom of our God, and the power of his Christ: for the accuser of our brethren is cast down, which accused them before our God day and night. ¹¹ And they overcame him by the blood of the Lamb, and by the word of their testimony; and they loved not their lives unto the death. ¹² Therefore rejoice, ye heavens, and ye that dwell in them. Woe to the inhabiters of the earth and of the sea! for the devil is come down unto you, having great wrath, because he knoweth that he hath but a short time. ¹³ And when the dragon saw that he was cast unto the earth, he persecuted the woman which brought forth the man child. ¹⁴ And to the woman were given two wings of a great eagle, that she might fly into the wilderness, into her place, where she is nourished for a time, and times, and half a time, from the face of the serpent. ¹⁵ And the serpent cast out of his mouth water as a flood after the woman, that he might cause her to be carried away of the flood. ¹⁶ And the earth helped the woman, and the earth opened her mouth, and swallowed up the flood which the dragon cast out of his mouth. ¹⁷ And the dragon was wroth with the woman, and went to make war with the remnant of her seed, which keep the commandments of God, and have the testimony of Jesus Christ.

Revelation 13

¹ And I stood upon the sand of the sea, and saw a beast rise up out of the sea, having seven heads and ten horns, and upon his horns ten crowns, and upon his heads the name of blasphemy. ² And the beast which I saw was like unto a leopard, and his feet were as the feet of a bear, and his mouth as the mouth of a lion: and the dragon gave him his power, and his seat, and great authority. ³ And I saw one of his heads as it were wounded to death; and his deadly wound was healed: and all the world wondered after the beast. ⁴ And they worshipped the dragon which gave power unto the beast: and they worshipped the beast, saying, Who is like unto the beast? who is able to make war with him? ⁵ And there was given unto him a mouth speaking great things and blasphemies; and power was given unto him to continue forty and two months. ⁶ And he opened his mouth in blasphemy against God, to blaspheme his name, and his tabernacle, and them that dwell in heaven. ⁷ And it was given unto him to make war with the saints, and to overcome them: and power was given him over all kindreds, and tongues, and nations. ⁸ And all that dwell upon the earth shall worship him, whose names are not written in the book of life of the Lamb slain from the foundation of the world. ⁹ If any man have an ear, let him hear. ¹⁰ He that leadeth into captivity shall go into captivity: he that killeth with the sword must be killed with the sword. Here is the patience and the faith of the saints. ¹¹ And I beheld another beast coming up out of the earth; and he had two horns like a lamb, and he spake as a dragon. ¹² And he exerciseth all the power of the first beast before him, and causeth the earth and them which dwell therein to worship the first beast, whose deadly wound was healed. ¹³ And he doeth great wonders, so that he maketh fire come down

from heaven on the earth in the sight of men, [14] And deceiveth them that dwell on the earth by the means of those miracles which he had power to do in the sight of the beast; saying to them that dwell on the earth, that they should make an image to the beast, which had the wound by a sword, and did live. [15] And he had power to give life unto the image of the beast, that the image of the beast should both speak, and cause that as many as would not worship the image of the beast should be killed. [16] And he causeth all, both small and great, rich and poor, free and bond, to receive a mark in their right hand, or in their foreheads: [17] And that no man might buy or sell, save he that had the mark, or the name of the beast, or the number of his name. [18] Here is wisdom. Let him that hath understanding count the number of the beast: for it is the number of a man; and his number is Six hundred threescore and six.

Revelation 14

[1] And I looked, and, lo, a Lamb stood on the mount Sion, and with him an hundred forty and four thousand, having his Father's name written in their foreheads. [2] And I heard a voice from heaven, as the voice of many waters, and as the voice of a great thunder: and I heard the voice of harpers harping with their harps: [3] And they sung as it were a new song before the throne, and before the four beasts, and the elders: and no man could learn that song but the hundred and forty and four thousand, which were redeemed from the earth. [4] These are they which were not defiled with women; for they are virgins. These are they which follow the Lamb whithersoever he goeth. These were redeemed from among men, being the firstfruits unto God and to the Lamb. [5] And in their mouth was found no guile: for they are without fault before the throne of God. [6] And I saw another angel fly in the midst of heaven, having the everlasting

gospel to preach unto them that dwell on the earth, and to every nation, and kindred, and tongue, and people, [7] Saying with a loud voice, Fear God, and give glory to him; for the hour of his judgment is come: and worship him that made heaven, and earth, and the sea, and the fountains of waters. [8] And there followed another angel, saying, Babylon is fallen, is fallen, that great city, because she made all nations drink of the wine of the wrath of her fornication. [9] And the third angel followed them, saying with a loud voice, If any man worship the beast and his image, and receive his mark in his forehead, or in his hand, [10] The same shall drink of the wine of the wrath of God, which is poured out without mixture into the cup of his indignation; and he shall be tormented with fire and brimstone in the presence of the holy angels, and in the presence of the Lamb: [11] And the smoke of their torment ascendeth up for ever and ever: and they have no rest day nor night, who worship the beast and his image, and whosoever receiveth the mark of his name. [12] Here is the patience of the saints: here are they that keep the commandments of God, and the faith of Jesus. [13] And I heard a voice from heaven saying unto me, Write, Blessed are the dead which die in the Lord from henceforth: Yea, saith the Spirit, that they may rest from their labours; and their works do follow them. [14] And I looked, and behold a white cloud, and upon the cloud one sat like unto the Son of man, having on his head a golden crown, and in his hand a sharp sickle. [15] And another angel came out of the temple, crying with a loud voice to him that sat on the cloud, Thrust in thy sickle, and reap: for the time is come for thee to reap; for the harvest of the earth is ripe. [16] And he that sat on the cloud thrust in his sickle on the earth; and the earth was reaped. [17] And another angel came out of the temple which is in heaven, he also having a sharp sickle. [18]

And another angel came out from the altar, which had power over fire; and cried with a loud cry to him that had the sharp sickle, saying, Thrust in thy sharp sickle, and gather the clusters of the vine of the earth; for her grapes are fully ripe. [19] And the angel thrust in his sickle into the earth, and gathered the vine of the earth, and cast it into the great winepress of the wrath of God. [20] And the winepress was trodden without the city, and blood came out of the winepress, even unto the horse bridles, by the space of a thousand and six hundred furlongs.

Revelation 15

[1] And I saw another sign in heaven, great and marvellous, seven angels having the seven last plagues; for in them is filled up the wrath of God. [2] And I saw as it were a sea of glass mingled with fire: and them that had gotten the victory over the beast, and over his image, and over his mark, and over the number of his name, stand on the sea of glass, having the harps of God. [3] And they sing the song of Moses the servant of God, and the song of the Lamb, saying, Great and marvellous are thy works, Lord God Almighty; just and true are thy ways, thou King of saints. [4] Who shall not fear thee, O Lord, and glorify thy name? for thou only art holy: for all nations shall come and worship before thee; for thy judgments are made manifest. [5] And after that I looked, and, behold, the temple of the tabernacle of the testimony in heaven was opened: [6] And the seven angels came out of the temple, having the seven plagues, clothed in pure and white linen, and having their breasts girded with golden girdles. [7] And one of the four beasts gave unto the seven angels seven golden vials full of the wrath of God, who liveth for ever and ever. [8] And the temple was filled with smoke from the glory of

God, and from his power; and no man was able to enter into the temple, till the seven plagues of the seven angels were fulfilled.

Revelation 16

¹ And I heard a great voice out of the temple saying to the seven angels, Go your ways, and pour out the vials of the wrath of God upon the earth. ² And the first went, and poured out his vial upon the earth; and there fell a noisome and grievous sore upon the men which had the mark of the beast, and upon them which worshipped his image. ³ And the second angel poured out his vial upon the sea; and it became as the blood of a dead man: and every living soul died in the sea. ⁴ And the third angel poured out his vial upon the rivers and fountains of waters; and they became blood. ⁵ And I heard the angel of the waters say, Thou art righteous, O Lord, which art, and wast, and shalt be, because thou hast judged thus. ⁶ For they have shed the blood of saints and prophets, and thou hast given them blood to drink; for they are worthy. ⁷ And I heard another out of the altar say, Even so, Lord God Almighty, true and righteous are thy judgments. ⁸ And the fourth angel poured out his vial upon the sun; and power was given unto him to scorch men with fire. ⁹ And men were scorched with great heat, and blasphemed the name of God, which hath power over these plagues: and they repented not to give him glory. ¹⁰ And the fifth angel poured out his vial upon the seat of the beast; and his kingdom was full of darkness; and they gnawed their tongues for pain, ¹¹ And blasphemed the God of heaven because of their pains and their sores, and repented not of their deeds. ¹² And the sixth angel poured out his vial upon the great river Euphrates; and the water thereof was dried up, that the way of the kings of the east might be prepared. ¹³ And I saw three unclean spirits like frogs come out of the mouth of the dragon,

and out of the mouth of the beast, and out of the mouth of the false prophet. [14] For they are the spirits of devils, working miracles, which go forth unto the kings of the earth and of the whole world, to gather them to the battle of that great day of God Almighty. [15] Behold, I come as a thief. Blessed is he that watcheth, and keepeth his garments, lest he walk naked, and they see his shame. [16] And he gathered them together into a place called in the Hebrew tongue Armageddon. [17] And the seventh angel poured out his vial into the air; and there came a great voice out of the temple of heaven, from the throne, saying, It is done. [18] And there were voices, and thunders, and lightnings; and there was a great earthquake, such as was not since men were upon the earth, so mighty an earthquake, and so great. [19] And the great city was divided into three parts, and the cities of the nations fell: and great Babylon came in remembrance before God, to give unto her the cup of the wine of the fierceness of his wrath. [20] And every island fled away, and the mountains were not found. [21] And there fell upon men a great hail out of heaven, every stone about the weight of a talent: and men blasphemed God because of the plague of the hail; for the plague thereof was exceeding great.

Revelation 17

[1] And there came one of the seven angels which had the seven vials, and talked with me, saying unto me, Come hither; I will shew unto thee the judgment of the great whore that sitteth upon many waters: [2] With whom the kings of the earth have committed fornication, and the inhabitants of the earth have been made drunk with the wine of her fornication. [3] So he carried me away in the spirit into the wilderness: and I saw a woman sit upon a scarlet coloured beast, full of names of blasphemy, having seven heads and

ten horns. [4] And the woman was arrayed in purple and scarlet co-
lour, and decked with gold and precious stones and pearls, having
a golden cup in her hand full of abominations and filthiness of her
fornication: [5] And upon her forehead was a name written, MYS-
TERY, BABYLON THE GREAT, THE MOTHER OF HARLOTS AND ABOMI-
NATIONS OF THE EARTH. [6] And I saw the woman drunken with the
blood of the saints, and with the blood of the martyrs of Jesus:
and when I saw her, I wondered with great admiration. [7] And the
angel said unto me, Wherefore didst thou marvel? I will tell thee
the mystery of the woman, and of the beast that carrieth her, which
hath the seven heads and ten horns. [8] The beast that thou sawest
was, and is not; and shall ascend out of the bottomless pit, and
go into perdition: and they that dwell on the earth shall wonder,
whose names were not written in the book of life from the foundation of the world, when they behold the beast that was, and is not,
and yet is. [9] And here is the mind which hath wisdom. The seven
heads are seven mountains, on which the woman sitteth. [10] And
there are seven kings: five are fallen, and one is, and the other is not
yet come; and when he cometh, he must continue a short space.
[11] And the beast that was, and is not, even he is the eighth, and is
of the seven, and goeth into perdition. [12] And the ten horns which
thou sawest are ten kings, which have received no kingdom as yet;
but receive power as kings one hour with the beast. [13] These have
one mind, and shall give their power and strength unto the beast. [14]
These shall make war with the Lamb, and the Lamb shall overcome
them: for he is Lord of lords, and King of kings: and they that
are with him are called, and chosen, and faithful. [15] And he saith
unto me, The waters which thou sawest, where the whore sitteth,
are peoples, and multitudes, and nations, and tongues. [16] And the

ten horns which thou sawest upon the beast, these shall hate the whore, and shall make her desolate and naked, and shall eat her flesh, and burn her with fire. [17] For God hath put in their hearts to fulfil his will, and to agree, and give their kingdom unto the beast, until the words of God shall be fulfilled. [18] And the woman which thou sawest is that great city, which reigneth over the kings of the earth.

Revelation 18

[1] And after these things I saw another angel come down from heaven, having great power; and the earth was lightened with his glory. [2] And he cried mightily with a strong voice, saying, Babylon the great is fallen, is fallen, and is become the habitation of devils, and the hold of every foul spirit, and a cage of every unclean and hateful bird. [3] For all nations have drunk of the wine of the wrath of her fornication, and the kings of the earth have committed fornication with her, and the merchants of the earth are waxed rich through the abundance of her delicacies. [4] And I heard another voice from heaven, saying, Come out of her, my people, that ye be not partakers of her sins, and that ye receive not of her plagues. [5] For her sins have reached unto heaven, and God hath remembered her iniquities. [6] Reward her even as she rewarded you, and double unto her double according to her works: in the cup which she hath filled fill to her double. [7] How much she hath glorified herself, and lived deliciously, so much torment and sorrow give her: for she saith in her heart, I sit a queen, and am no widow, and shall see no sorrow. [8] Therefore shall her plagues come in one day, death, and mourning, and famine; and she shall be utterly burned with fire: for strong is the Lord God who judgeth her. [9] And the kings of the earth, who have committed fornication and lived deliciously with

her, shall bewail her, and lament for her, when they shall see the smoke of her burning, [10] Standing afar off for the fear of her torment, saying, Alas, alas that great city Babylon, that mighty city! for in one hour is thy judgment come. [11] And the merchants of the earth shall weep and mourn over her; for no man buyeth their merchandise any more: [12] The merchandise of gold, and silver, and precious stones, and of pearls, and fine linen, and purple, and silk, and scarlet, and all thyine wood, and all manner vessels of ivory, and all manner vessels of most precious wood, and of brass, and iron, and marble, [13] And cinnamon, and odours, and ointments, and frankincense, and wine, and oil, and fine flour, and wheat, and beasts, and sheep, and horses, and chariots, and slaves, and souls of men. [14] And the fruits that thy soul lusted after are departed from thee, and all things which were dainty and goodly are departed from thee, and thou shalt find them no more at all. [15] The merchants of these things, which were made rich by her, shall stand afar off for the fear of her torment, weeping and wailing, [16] And saying, Alas, alas that great city, that was clothed in fine linen, and purple, and scarlet, and decked with gold, and precious stones, and pearls! [17] For in one hour so great riches is come to nought. And every shipmaster, and all the company in ships, and sailors, and as many as trade by sea, stood afar off, [18] And cried when they saw the smoke of her burning, saying, What city is like unto this great city! [19] And they cast dust on their heads, and cried, weeping and wailing, saying, Alas, alas that great city, wherein were made rich all that had ships in the sea by reason of her costliness! for in one hour is she made desolate. [20] Rejoice over her, thou heaven, and ye holy apostles and prophets; for God hath avenged you on her. [21] And a mighty angel took up a stone like a great millstone, and cast it into the sea, saying, Thus with violence shall that great city Babylon be thrown down, and shall be found no more at all. [22] And the voice of harpers, and musicians, and of pipers, and trumpeters, shall be heard no more at all in thee; and no craftsman, of whatsoever craft he be, shall be found any more in thee; and the sound of a millstone shall be heard no more at all in thee; [23] And the light of a candle shall shine no more at all in thee; and the voice of the bridegroom and of the bride shall be heard no more at all in thee: for thy merchants were the great men of the earth; for by thy sorceries were all nations deceived. [24] And in her was found the blood of prophets, and of saints, and of all that were slain upon the earth.

Revelation 19

[1] And after these things I heard a great voice of much people in heaven, saying, Alleluia; Salvation, and glory, and honour, and power, unto the Lord our God: [2] For true and righteous are his judgments: for he hath judged the great whore, which did corrupt the earth with her fornication, and hath avenged the blood of his servants at her hand. [3] And again they said, Alleluia And her smoke rose up for ever and ever. [4] And the four and twenty elders and the four beasts fell down and worshipped God that sat on the throne, saying, Amen; Alleluia. [5] And a voice came out of the throne, saying, Praise our God, all ye his servants, and ye that fear him, both small and great. [6] And I heard as it were the voice of a great multitude, and as the voice of many waters, and as the voice of mighty thunderings, saying, Alleluia: for the Lord God omnipotent reigneth. [7] Let us be glad and rejoice, and give honour to him: for the marriage of the Lamb is come, and his wife hath made herself ready. [8] And to her was granted that she should be arrayed in fine linen, clean and white: for the fine linen is the righteousness

of saints. [9] And he saith unto me, Write, Blessed are they which are called unto the marriage supper of the Lamb. And he saith unto me, These are the true sayings of God. [10] And I fell at his feet to worship him. And he said unto me, See thou do it not: I am thy fellowservant, and of thy brethren that have the testimony of Jesus: worship God: for the testimony of Jesus is the spirit of prophecy. [11] And I saw heaven opened, and behold a white horse; and he that sat upon him was called Faithful and True, and in righteousness he doth judge and make war. [12] His eyes were as a flame of fire, and on his head were many crowns; and he had a name written, that no man knew, but he himself. [13] And he was clothed with a vesture dipped in blood: and his name is called The Word of God. [14] And the armies which were in heaven followed him upon white horses, clothed in fine linen, white and clean. [15] And out of his mouth goeth a sharp sword, that with it he should smite the nations: and he shall rule them with a rod of iron: and he treadeth the winepress of the fierceness and wrath of Almighty God. [16] And he hath on his vesture and on his thigh a name written, KING OF KINGS, AND LORD OF LORDS. [17] And I saw an angel standing in the sun; and he cried with a loud voice, saying to all the fowls that fly in the midst of heaven, Come and gather yourselves together unto the supper of the great God; [18] That ye may eat the flesh of kings, and the flesh of captains, and the flesh of mighty men, and the flesh of horses, and of them that sit on them, and the flesh of all men, both free and bond, both small and great. [19] And I saw the beast, and the kings of the earth, and their armies, gathered together to make war against him that sat on the horse, and against his army. [20] And the beast was taken, and with him the false prophet that wrought miracles before him, with which he deceived them that had received the mark of the beast, and them that worshipped his image. These both were cast alive into a lake of fire burning with brimstone. [21] And the remnant were slain with the sword of him that sat upon the horse, which sword proceeded out of his mouth: and all the fowls were filled with their flesh.

Revelation 20

[1] And I saw an angel come down from heaven, having the key of the bottomless pit and a great chain in his hand. [2] And he laid hold on the dragon, that old serpent, which is the Devil, and Satan, and bound him a thousand years, [3] And cast him into the bottomless pit, and shut him up, and set a seal upon him, that he should deceive the nations no more, till the thousand years should be fulfilled: and after that he must be loosed a little season. [4] And I saw thrones, and they sat upon them, and judgment was given unto them: and I saw the souls of them that were beheaded for the witness of Jesus, and for the word of God, and which had not worshipped the beast, neither his image, neither had received his mark upon their foreheads, or in their hands; and they lived and reigned with Christ a thousand years. [5] But the rest of the dead lived not again until the thousand years were finished. This is the first resurrection. [6] Blessed and holy is he that hath part in the first resurrection: on such the second death hath no power, but they shall be priests of God and of Christ, and shall reign with him a thousand years. [7] And when the thousand years are expired, Satan shall be loosed out of his prison, [8] And shall go out to deceive the nations which are in the four quarters of the earth, Gog, and Magog, to gather them together to battle: the number of whom is as the sand of the sea. [9] And they went up on the breadth of the earth, and compassed the camp of the saints about, and the beloved city:

and fire came down from God out of heaven, and devoured them.
[10] And the devil that deceived them was cast into the lake of fire
and brimstone, where the beast and the false prophet are, and shall
be tormented day and night for ever and ever. [11] And I saw a great
white throne, and him that sat on it, from whose face the earth
and the heaven fled away; and there was found no place for them.
[12] And I saw the dead, small and great, stand before God; and the
books were opened: and another book was opened, which is the
book of life: and the dead were judged out of those things which
were written in the books, according to their works. [13] And the sea
gave up the dead which were in it; and death and hell delivered up
the dead which were in them: and they were judged every man according to their works. [14] And death and hell were cast into the lake
of fire. This is the second death. [15] And whosoever was not found
written in the book of life was cast into the lake of fire.

Revelation 21

[1] And I saw a new heaven and a new earth: for the first heaven and
the first earth were passed away; and there was no more sea. [2] And
I John saw the holy city, new Jerusalem, coming down from God
out of heaven, prepared as a bride adorned for her husband. [3] And
I heard a great voice out of heaven saying, Behold, the tabernacle
of God is with men, and he will dwell with them, and they shall be
his people, and God himself shall be with them, and be their God.
[4] And God shall wipe away all tears from their eyes; and there shall
be no more death, neither sorrow, nor crying, neither shall there be
any more pain: for the former things are passed away. [5] And he that
sat upon the throne said, Behold, I make all things new. And he said
unto me, Write: for these words are true and faithful. [6] And he said
unto me, It is done. I am Alpha and Omega, the beginning and the

end. I will give unto him that is athirst of the fountain of the water of life freely. [7] He that overcometh shall inherit all things; and I will be his God, and he shall be my son. [8] But the fearful, and unbelieving, and the abominable, and murderers, and whoremongers, and sorcerers, and idolaters, and all liars, shall have their part in the lake which burneth with fire and brimstone: which is the second death. [9] And there came unto me one of the seven angels which had the seven vials full of the seven last plagues, and talked with me, saying, Come hither, I will shew thee the bride, the Lamb's wife. [10] And he carried me away in the spirit to a great and high mountain, and shewed me that great city, the holy Jerusalem, descending out of heaven from God, [11] Having the glory of God: and her light was like unto a stone most precious, even like a jasper stone, clear as crystal; [12] And had a wall great and high, and had twelve gates, and at the gates twelve angels, and names written thereon, which are the names of the twelve tribes of the children of Israel: [13] On the east three gates; on the north three gates; on the south three gates; and on the west three gates. [14] And the wall of the city had twelve foundations, and in them the names of the twelve apostles of the Lamb. [15] And he that talked with me had a golden reed to measure the city, and the gates thereof, and the wall thereof. [16] And the city lieth foursquare, and the length is as large as the breadth: and he measured the city with the reed, twelve thousand furlongs. The length and the breadth and the height of it are equal. [17] And he measured the wall thereof, an hundred and forty and four cubits, according to the measure of a man, that is, of the angel. [18] And the building of the wall of it was of jasper: and the city was pure gold, like unto clear glass. [19] And the foundations of the wall of the city were garnished with all manner of precious stones. The first foundation was jasper; the second, sapphire; the third, a chalcedony; the fourth, an emerald; [20] The fifth, sardonyx; the sixth, sardius; the seventh, chrysolyte; the eighth, beryl; the ninth, a topaz; the tenth, a chrysoprasus; the eleventh, a jacinth; the twelfth, an amethyst. [21] And the twelve gates were twelve pearls: every several gate was of one pearl: and the street of the city was pure gold, as it were transparent glass. [22] And I saw no temple therein: for the Lord God Almighty and the Lamb are the temple of it. [23] And the city had no need of the sun, neither of the moon, to shine in it: for the glory of God did lighten it, and the Lamb is the light thereof. [24] And the nations of them which are saved shall walk in the light of it: and the kings of the earth do bring their glory and honour into it. [25] And the gates of it shall not be shut at all by day: for there shall be no night there. [26] And they shall bring the glory and honour of the nations into it. [27] And there shall in no wise enter into it any thing that defileth, neither whatsoever worketh abomination, or maketh a lie: but they which are written in the Lamb's book of life.

Revelation 22

[1] And he shewed me a pure river of water of life, clear as crystal, proceeding out of the throne of God and of the Lamb. [2] In the midst of the street of it, and on either side of the river, was there the tree of life, which bare twelve manner of fruits, and yielded her fruit every month: and the leaves of the tree were for the healing of the nations. [3] And there shall be no more curse: but the throne of God and of the Lamb shall be in it; and his servants shall serve him: [4] And they shall see his face; and his name shall be in their foreheads. [5] And there shall be no night there; and they need no candle, neither light of the sun; for the Lord God giveth them light: and they shall reign for ever and ever. [6] And he said unto me,

These sayings are faithful and true: and the Lord God of the holy prophets sent his angel to shew unto his servants the things which must shortly be done. [7] Behold, I come quickly: blessed is he that keepeth the sayings of the prophecy of this book. [8] And I John saw these things, and heard them. And when I had heard and seen, I fell down to worship before the feet of the angel which shewed me these things. [9] Then saith he unto me, See thou do it not: for I am thy fellowservant, and of thy brethren the prophets, and of them which keep the sayings of this book: worship God. [10] And he saith unto me, Seal not the sayings of the prophecy of this book: for the time is at hand. [11] He that is unjust, let him be unjust still: and he which is filthy, let him be filthy still: and he that is righteous, let him be righteous still: and he that is holy, let him be holy still. [12] And, behold, I come quickly; and my reward is with me, to give every man according as his work shall be. [13] I am Alpha and Omega, the beginning and the end, the first and the last. [14] Blessed are they that do his commandments, that they may have right to the tree of life, and may enter in through the gates into the city. [15] For without are dogs, and sorcerers, and whoremongers, and mur-derers, and idolaters, and whosoever loveth and maketh a lie. [16] I Jesus have sent mine angel to testify unto you these things in the churches. I am the root and the offspring of David, and the bright and morning star. [17] And the Spirit and the bride say, Come. And let him that heareth say, Come. And let him that is athirst come. And whosoever will, let him take the water of life freely. [18] For I testify unto every man that heareth the words of the prophecy of this book, If any man shall add unto these things, God shall add unto him the plagues that are written in this book: [19] And if any man shall take away from the words of the book of this prophecy,

God shall take away his part out of the book of life, and out of the holy city, and from the things which are written in this book. [20] He which testifieth these things saith, Surely I come quickly. Amen. Even so, come, Lord Jesus. [21] The grace of our Lord Jesus Christ be with you all. Amen.

Recommended Reading

The technical name for the study of prophecy regarding the last days is "Eschatology." There are many good books by different authors on the subject. These can be found in most Christian bookshops.

By far the best and most informed study on the Book of Revelation was written about one hundred years ago. It is a mine of information and quite simple to read. It is:

Bullinger, E. W. (1984) *Commentary on Revelation*. Grand Rapids, MI: Kregal Publications.

Other Reading:

De Haan, M. R. (1962) *Coming Events in Prophecy*. Grand Rapids, MI: Zondervan Publishing House.

Lalonde, Peter and Patti. (1995) *Left Behind*. Eugene, OR: Harvest House Publishers.

Larkin, Clarence. (1918) *Dispensational Truth or God's Plan and Purpose for the Ages*. Glenside, PA.

Lindsey, Hal. (1994) *Planet Earth - 2000 AD—Will Mankind Survive?*. Palos Verdes, CA: Western Front Ltd.

Pentecost, J. Dwight (1980) *Will Man Survive? The Bible Looks at Man's Future*. Grand Rapids, MI: Zondervan Publishing House.

About the Author

Patrick Heron has studied the Bible for over thirty years.. He received his BSc. and MA in Business Studies from Trinity College Dublin and also has a Degree in Theology. Recently he was awarded an Honorary Doctorate in Christian Literature from the California Pacific School of Theology as a result of the research done in his book *The Nephilim and the Pyramid of the Apocalypse*. Married with three children, he has a successful business in Dublin.

"When I was twenty-four I had a spiritual experience one night while reading the Bible. Just like Saul on the road to Damascus, I 'saw the light' and came to a personal knowledge of Jesus Christ and the Word of God. That night I believe God told me that I would be alive at the moment Jesus Christ comes back. For thirty years I have been convinced of this. A number of years ago some friends and I started to read books on prophecy in the Bible concerning the 'End Times' or "Last Days.'

"When I discovered that what was prophesied was going to happen, I felt everybody should at least have the opportunity of hearing what was written. Jesus Christ gave us this prophecy. Whether you want to believe him or not is up to you. I have written this book so that ordinary people could get the chance to read it and decide for themselves.

"On the night I came to know Jesus Christ, I had a vision. I believe that vision will soon be a reality. I know God's hand has been on my life. I hope and pray that when you read this book you will see the truth and realise that Jesus Christ is alive and that what he said shall be, shall be."